Extraordinary
WOMEN

JULIE CLINTON
with MARY M. BYERS

HARVEST HOUSE PUBLISHERS

EUGENE, OREGON

EXTRAORDINARY WOMEN
Copyright © 2007 by Julie Clinton
Published by Harvest House Publishers
Eugene, Oregon 97402
www.harvesthousepublishers.com

Library of Congress Cataloging-in-Publication Data
   Clinton, Julie, 1961-
   Extraordinary women / Julie Clinton with Mary M. Byers.
     p. cm.
   ISBN 978-0-7369-2375-0 (pbk.)
   ISBN 978-0-7369-2110-7 (hardcover)
   1. Christian women—Religious life. I. Byers, Mary M., 1962- II. Title.
   BV4527.C57 2007
   248.8'43—dc22
                                          2007017288

To the women who hunger after God
and dare to be bold in their faith
and to the loving memory of my father
Clayton Ray Rothmann
(1938–2000)

Acknowledgments

Since I've been little, I've always wanted to write my thoughts and share my heart in words. But I had no idea what kind of effort writing a book like this would require! God has been so good to me! He has surrounded me with a wonderful, godly family while I was growing up, including a loving father who left this earth for heaven far too soon. I miss you, Dad, and I deeply appreciate your love and the life lessons you taught me.

I want to thank my heavenly Father for bringing into my life the people, the resources, and the opportunity to complete this work, and I offer it to Him for His glory.

A special thank you to Harvest House Publishers for your support and encouragement—especially to Terry Glaspey and Carolyn McCready for believing in me and this book.

Thanks to Mary Byers for teaming up with me and diligently assisting with the writing of this book. I love your heart and passion for women!

Likewise, a special thank you to (soon to be Dr.) Joshua Straub for the many long hours in research, writing, and editing.

To Tom Winters, and his assistant, Debbie Boyd, a huge thank-you for introducing me to the wonderful world of publishing.

Thanks to the women who filled these pages with heartfelt stories of their love for life.

To team Extraordinary Women, God is awakening the hearts of women to do His good work all over America. The best is yet to be!

Thanks to my mother, who faithfully prays for me and has taught me the holy Scriptures since I was little.

And to my loving husband, Tim, and to our two children, Megan and Zach—you bring so much joy to my life.

Contents

Foreword

I first met Julie Clinton at an Extraordinary Women conference. Her passion for God and her deep desire to point women to an eternal perspective instantly bonded my heart to hers. She is an extraordinary woman of influence for God's glory. I know her spiritual authenticity, her knowledge of God's Word, and her commonsense practical applications throughout this book will provide you and thousands of other women the life lessons and practical how-tos we all long to know in order to be more effective Christian women.

As a teenager I told God I wanted to live for things that mattered. I wanted to come to the end of my life knowing I had lived with purpose, with conviction, and with a heart determined to follow His call, regardless of where it took me. At that time I thought my commitment might mean overseas missions or perhaps teaching highly motivated students. I didn't know that path would lead me to writing books and speaking at women's conferences. As I've followed His call, I've learned that life is not always idyllic, tranquil, and without problems. But this book teaches you how to be an extraordinary woman even when circumstances are less than ideal.

As you read, you'll learn how the supernatural person of Christ gives us the ability to see with different eyes, to perceive purpose and meaning in the middle of our daily, imperfect, and disappointing life experiences. Julie has unlocked the secrets to capturing the dream God has in mind for you. This dream may not look like the one you once wrote on a goal chart with carefully developed smaller steps that led to the big picture. The real secret of this dream is that God looks at you, flaws and all, and says, "'For I know the plans I have for you,' says the LORD. 'They are plans for good and not for disaster, to give you a future and a hope'" (Jeremiah 29:11 NLT).

Thinking of yourself as an extraordinary woman might seem arrogant to you, but that's how God designed you. You are a one-of-a-kind woman with a distinct personality, unique gifts, and the potential to make a mark in this world that is different from any other. God loves you with an everlasting love, and He will never walk away from you. Unlike many people you've encountered, He offers a love that is sticky, resistant to rejection, longsuffering, and pure.

Extraordinary women have many things in common. They look at the world differently. Instead of seeing roadblocks, they visualize the finish line. They replace negativism with optimism. They instinctively realize that problems are solvable and that difficult people are rarely "out to get them"—they're just struggling with their own issues. Extraordinary women know how to dream beyond their current challenging circumstances and believe God has a plan for them that surpasses the finest scenario they could imagine.

The book is uniquely designed to teach you how to embrace God's love, discover His purpose for your life, develop meaningful relationships, understand men, get through tough times, and live with passion, balance, purpose, and joy. The surprising truth is that extraordinary women don't necessarily live easy, uncomplicated, predictable, and financially wealthy lives. But they do respond in extraordinary ways when life hands them extraordinarily difficult circumstances. (You'll learn about my own challenge in this regard when you read my story, which begins on page 161.)

This book gives you opportunities to write out your thoughts, meditate on biblical truth, dialogue with God and others, and make new decisions about how you will live for things that matter. As you grow in your faith, you will discover how to capture the dream God has for you.

Extraordinary women go beyond what is usual, regular, or customary. As Christian women, we have the "real" secret: the supernatural power of God Himself invading our lives with His desires. In the process of loving Him and following His heart, we get balance, vision, and everything we need to fulfill His call on our lives. I hope you will encourage other women to experience this book with you as you learn how to become an extraordinary woman of God.

Carol Kent, author of
When I Lay My Isaac Down (NavPress)
A New Kind of Normal (Thomas Nelson)

Introduction

"Why do we try so hard to fit in when God created us to stand out?"

My 17-year-old daughter, Megan, was chosen this past year to be one of five candidates on the Winterfest court held at her school. Winterfest is similar to homecoming except five juniors are chosen and crowned at halftime of a basketball game instead of a football game. The day before the crowning, each contestant delivers a challenge to the student body. As Megan and I cuddled on the couch, preparing her speech the night before, we got on the topic of God's dream for our lives. We talked about His plans versus our desires, His love versus our mistakes. As we lay talking about God, life, school, and boys, Megan stopped. She looked me in the eyes and asked the question I just raised to you.

At home on that cold January evening, my daughter challenged me. And as I pondered the question, I realized life is not about drawing attention to ourselves and what we do. It's about drawing attention to Him and lifting Him up. Even Jesus declared, "I am not seeking glory for myself; but there is one who seeks it, and He is the judge" (John 8:50).

As you read through the pages that follow, understand and constantly remind yourself of this truth: God loves His daughters. That's right, God loves *you*. And He is in the business of making *you* extraordinary.

How do I know? Prior to His death and resurrection, Jesus promised the disciples He would send the Holy Spirit to them.

> If you love me, show it by doing what I've told you. I will talk to the Father, and he'll provide you another Friend so that you

will always have someone with you. This Friend is the Spirit of Truth. The godless world can't take Him in because it doesn't have eyes to see Him, doesn't know what to look for. But you know Him already because He has been staying with you, and will even be in you! (John 14:15-17 MSG).

The promise Jesus made to His disciples so long ago is still relevant to His disciples today. The Friend, Counselor, and Helper Jesus promised to send resides in you at this very moment. This Spirit of Truth is the same Spirit that enables ordinary women—like you and me—to become extraordinary.

In this book you'll read about women who've had extraordinary encounters with Christ. You'll meet everyday women who are using their passion and skills to make an unimaginable impact in the world. You'll learn about regular women who are allowing God to use them in the midst of trying circumstances. And most importantly, you'll be challenged to ask yourself how you can actively work with the Holy Spirit to complete your own personal transformation into an extraordinary woman.

Some of what you read might be unsettling. Some may cause you to question your own motives and decisions. That's purposeful. I want you to be challenged as you read. I know you are interested in being the best you can be for your family, your church, your community, and God. Sometimes that means taking a close look at yourself and deciding what and how you need to change.

Life is all about change. It's a process I've been through, am going through, and will continue to go through for the rest of my life. I'll share with you a little about my journey in this regard as we move through the pages of this book together.

In addition to learning about the power of the Holy Spirit that resides in you, we'll be learning the secrets of extraordinary women. By my dictionary's definition, secrets are "beyond general understanding; mysterious; concealed from sight and hidden." With a little help from the Holy Spirit, however, I believe we can uncover these secrets, thereby tapping into their power.

I've designed this book as a ten-week study. Each chapter is intended to take a week, with five daily readings each revealing a secret. Look for Live the Dream at the end of each reading, which summarizes what extraordinary women know, do, and practice. You'll also find Journal Prompts—questions to get you started writing in your journal in order to help you learn more about yourself and what you need to do personally in order to bring the extraordinary into your life.

The daily readings are short so you can fit them into your busy daily schedule. But don't worry or get hung up if you get behind. Our time together isn't meant to be a chore or one more thing to add to your to-do list. Instead, I hope your reading time provides encouragement and refreshment each day as you tend to all the responsibilities that come with being an extraordinary woman in today's merciless society.

Everything in this book is designed to draw you closer to the heart of God, to those you love most dearly, and ultimately to the extraordinary power of the Holy Spirit. My hope is that your walk with the Lord and your relationships with those you love will be deepened with every page. If so, you'll be well on your way to living the extraordinary life God has prepared for you. It's time to stand out!

Blessings,
Julie Clinton

Week 1

Secrets to Living God's Dream for Your Life

Dreams...all girls grow up with special dreams, like becoming a princess—a Cinderella or Sleeping Beauty. We want to be chased. Rescued. Desired. Little girls often play house with dreams of finding someone who will love them and kiss their face, who will tell them how beautiful they are. Or they dream of becoming a special mom with little babies who will grow up and change the world.

Being special in someone's eyes matters to us. That's why I love Jeremiah 29:11 (MSG): "I know what I'm doing. I have it all planned out—plans to take care of you, not abandon you, plans to give you the future you hope for." The Dream Giver Himself has a dream with *your* name on it. He always has. He's been dreaming about *you* since before you were born. And because He loves you with "an everlasting love" (Jeremiah 31:3), His dream for you is bigger and better than the one you have for yourself! He wants to use you for His glory.

The tragedy in life is that our dreams often get tarnished at the hands of life and other people. In fact, self-reported surveys show that up to 80 percent of people are not living out their dreams.

It's no secret that God has a plan for your life, but the details of His plan and the way you are to live it out may be secrets to you. God's plan may feel like a mystery, but God doesn't mean for it to be. In fact, He intends for you to determine what His dream is for you and to live it fully and abundantly.

This chapter is designed to entice you with the possibility of living God's dream for your life, to help you understand why it is important to God that you do, to assure you that God can use you where you are right now, and to encourage you to focus on what you're good at when it comes to doing kingdom work.

Day 1

Life Is More than Just Getting By

Dream as if you'll live forever;
live as if you'll die today.
JAMES DEAN

Are you going to merely live? Or are you going to live your dreams? These are questions that every woman must ask herself and answer at some point in life. If you haven't asked yourself these questions, now is the time. How you answer them will determine what the rest of your life will look like, starting today.

The difference between merely living and living your dreams is greater than you might think. Merely living includes behaviors like these:

- Going through the motions without much thought or concern for the future
- Getting through the day without carefully noticing how you spend your precious time
- Trudging through each week and month without any joy or peace
- Ignoring the areas of your life that cause you pain
- Assuming you don't really have the power to change your life—or your response to it

Living your dreams includes much more intentional actions:

- ☙ Taking the time to identify what God wants you to do and then making plans to do it

- ☙ Allocating your time in a way that helps you meet your needs as well as the needs of those around you

- ☙ Embracing the joy and peace that a relationship with Christ offers

- ☙ Acknowledging and addressing the issues that cause you pain

- ☙ Learning how to let the Holy Spirit work in you and through you so you can live more abundantly

Every day I get the chance to meet with, talk with, and work with exceptional women from all walks of life. Some are married, and some are not. Some are parents, and some are not. Some work outside the home, and some work from it. Some run marathons, and some are challenged by chronic illness or pain. Some have gotten everything they wanted in life, and some have not. Most fit into more than one of these categories. But all have made the same decision: They choose to live life fully and abundantly, the way Jesus wants them to. Jesus says, "I came so they can have real and eternal life, more and better life than they ever dreamed of" (John 10:10 MSG).

Some people may say that circumstances determine whether you can live out your dreams, but I disagree. I've met women who are challenged by the most difficult situations and yet manage to live abundantly. Joni Eareckson Tada is a great example. She has learned to live life to the fullest despite a diving accident that left her paralyzed and completely dependent on a wheelchair. And I have met women who have it all and are living small, unhappy lives. The difference is not in the circumstances. The difference is in the attitude. And the only difference between a positive attitude and a negative attitude is the decision to choose one over the other.

Extraordinary women decide that they will hold onto and live their dreams regardless of their circumstances. In the weeks ahead you'll see that living your dreams requires making the decision to do so every single day. You cannot make this choice once for all time. You must make this choice every day—and then consciously choose again every time life throws you a curve ball. Consequently, I believe that a full life is *lived in the moment of decision*. Let me explain.

Extraordinary women decide that life's disappointments, whether unemployment, the marriage proposal that never came, or the promotion that was never awarded, will not dampen their enthusiasm. They decide to continue to do their best and work to become better, not bitter.

Extraordinary women decide that a husband's death, disability, or infidelity will not cause them to give up. They decide to bravely face their circumstances.

Extraordinary women decide that a child's illness, physical or emotional limitations, rebelliousness, or waywardness will not completely bury their gift of mothering. They decide to persevere in loving and praying for each of the children entrusted to them.

Extraordinary women decide that physical limitations or illness will not rob them of joy. They decide to find the silver lining (as sparse as it may be) in every cloud.

Extraordinary women decide that money or lack of it will not determine their level of happiness. They decide that money is simply a means to an end and not an end itself.

Extraordinary women decide not to dwell on what they do not have. They recognize what they do have and are grateful for it.

Extraordinary women decide not to be overwhelmed by the tough choices and life-changing decisions that they will be called to make. They call on the power of the Holy Spirit to help them make wise judgments.

In short, extraordinary women *decide*.

Life is lived in the moment of decision. What kinds of decisions have you made lately? More importantly, what kinds of decisions do you need to make?

Do you need to get out of any bad relationships? Set boundaries with friends and family members? Start new habits or drop old ones? Do you need to change jobs? Do your children need more (or less) discipline? Has your marriage grown stale?

You may not know the answers to these questions right now. But I hope you'll be challenged to think about them as we journey together. Ultimately, the questions you ask yourself or refuse to ask, and the decisions you make or refuse to make, will determine the quality of your life.

Life is more than just getting by. Ordinary women get by. Extraordinary women live life to the full, as Jesus desires. As you read on, I hope you will clearly see where your life is full and perhaps where it's not. I also hope that the secrets we explore will encourage you to see that you *can* have a full and abundant life rather than one that's characterized by emptiness and scarcity.

Jesus came so that you too can be an extraordinary woman. Read on to find out how.

Live the
DREAM

Extraordinary women decide to hold onto and live their dreams regardless of their circumstances.

JOURNAL
PROMPTS

- What did you dream of becoming when you were a little girl? Has that dream come true for you?

- What obstacles are holding you back from experiencing your dreams?

- What decisions do you need to make in the coming days and weeks that you can ask the Holy Spirit to help you fulfill?

Day 2

Something Bigger

*Be faithful in small things because it is in
them that your strength lies.*
MOTHER TERESA

Extraordinary women are faithful in the small things, and that enables
God to entrust more to them as they mature and grow in their faith.

I'm sure that noted Bible teacher Beth Moore didn't know what God
had in mind for her when she began leading Christian aerobics years ago.
Since then, God has called her out of her spandex and around the world
to teach His Word. She teaches a 700-member Sunday school class at her
church and hosts an interdenominational Tuesday night Bible study for
women in her city. She's also authored multiple books and Bible study cur-
riculums.

Allison Bottke was born and raised in Cleveland. She ran away from
home at the age of 15 and married a young man whose abuse nearly ended
her life. Divorced and a mother at the age of 16, her tenacious spirit saw her
through three decades of turmoil and addiction before she came to know
the Lord. Now she's the editor of the inspiring God Allows U-Turns non-
fiction book series.

Heather Whitestone McCallum lost her hearing due to a virus she con-
tracted at the age of 18 months. Though profoundly deaf, she studied hard
and graduated from public high school with a 3.6 GPA. Due to financial

hardships at home, she started competing in pageants in order to win scholarship money for college. She competed in the Miss Alabama contest three times before winning the title and heading to Atlantic City to be crowned Miss America. She was the first woman with a disability to do so. Since then, she has written two books and traveled extensively, sharing how Jesus' influence in her life is the key to her success.

What if God's dream for your life was something bigger than you ever imagined?

If you knew God had bigger plans for you than you have for yourself, how would that change things for you? Would it scare you? Make you nervous? Excite you? Energize you? Make you want to lay down and take a nap?

Thankfully, God doesn't reveal His plans for us all at once—as if Publisher's Clearing House came to your door with balloons and flowers and a big check for a million dollars. Most of us would be overwhelmed by that. Instead, God gently takes us by the hand and leads us, a little at a time, to the future that only He can see. By moving us along gently, He gives us the time we need to mature, to develop the skills we need for the work He's planned, and to get used to the idea that all that's happened in the past may in fact be part of His grand plan for us.

By revealing His plan a little at a time, God helps us adjust to the idea that His plan may be bigger than we ever imagined.

When I was growing up as a young girl in Montana, I never dreamed God had plans for me to be serving Him the way I am—as president of Extraordinary Women, an association committed to drawing women closer to the heart of God. (Visit Extraordinary Women online at www.ewomen.net.) Standing in front of audiences always unnerved me. It still does today. But I've had to learn that God's dream for my life did not necessarily match mine. I'm still amazed when I consider the way God blesses this ministry and empowers me to lead the team of wonderful people who make it all happen. God's dream for me was certainly bigger than the one I had for myself!

At one point, I planned to be a lawyer. Then I was going to be a doctor. I ended up as a math teacher. But that was the perfect preparation for the next stop on my journey. I became the executive director of the Liberty Godparent Home, a home for unwed mothers. In that capacity, I was in charge of budgeting, operations, policy making, funding, and other tasks. I also helped girls select adoptive parents for their unborn children. That too prepared me for what I'm now doing. And I believe that whatever you are doing now is perfect preparation for the future that only God can see.

Like me, Beverly LaHaye, author and chair of Concerned Women for America, did not envision what God had in mind for her. She shares, "I could never have dreamed that as an ordinary girl from an ordinary family I would one day testify before the Senate Judicial Committee in support of a nominee for Justice of the Supreme Court. Or that I would meet privately with three presidents of Central American countries to speak about helping their families. Or that I would be able to minister in seven different refugee camps over a five-year period during the Nicaraguan Sandinista war where the refugees fled to Costa Rica for safety."

In Matthew, Jesus shares a parable about a master who entrusts part of his treasure to three servants while he is away on a trip. When he returns, he calls the servants together to see what they've done with his money. Two have made the money grow; one simply hid the money for fear of losing it. The master commends the two who made the money grow and condemns the other. The master's commendation consists of these words: "Well done, good and faithful servant! You have been faithful with a few things; I will put you in charge of many things" (Matthew 25:21).

Beth Moore was faithful while she was teaching aerobics. Allison Bottke struggled through her own turnaround before becoming the poster girl for life-changing U-turns. Heather Whitestone McCallum took six years to correctly pronounce her last name, and now she can introduce herself as a child of the King.

These women were all faithful in the little things, and that led to them being entrusted with bigger things.

God's plan for your life is bigger than you can imagine. Ask Him today to start revealing it to you. I'm confident you'll be surprised by what He has planned. And I know it's better than anything you have imagined!

Live the
DREAM

*Be faithful in the small things, and God will entrust
more to you as you mature and grow in your faith.*

JOURNAL
PROMPTS

- Are you presently doing the task God has called you to do in this moment? Are you doing it to the best of your ability for Him, or do you simply do the minimum to get by?

- In what ways and areas of your life is God calling you to be faithful right now?

- When you begin to believe God has something big planned for your life, what changes will occur in the way you live?

Day 3

Beautiful in His Eyes

The King is enthralled by your beauty.
PSALM 45:11

While I was growing up, my dad always called me his little angel. I was beautiful in his eyes, and that made me feel special. And even though he died a few years ago, far too young in this life, I still wake up at night hearing his encouraging and compassionate voice. Do I miss him? Yes. Long for him? Yes. Am I encouraged by him? Always. In my heart and in my spirit.

I have taken a while to understand how much my heavenly Father loves me. He loves far more deeply than my earthly father ever could. We are precious in His sight.

I know sometimes this is hard to believe, especially if you don't feel beautiful or didn't have a dad telling you how beautiful you really are. You might be thinking, *Nothing is special about me.*

But I beg to differ. Everything about you is special. The way God made your eyes to see hurting people around you. The way you laugh. Your compassion and tenderness. God loves the way you cry out to Him when you are on your knees in prayer. The way you think. The gentle way you're able to encourage other people. Or the way you listen when those around you need to talk. How you're able to whip up dinner from scratch or bake 12 dozen cookies without breaking a sweat. Your willingness to work in the nursery at church when no one else wants to. Your ability to comfort the grieving. Your courage in making tough decisions in the face of adversity.

You are precious in His eyes because He created you a certain way, with matchless abilities and special gifts. *You* are wonderfully made and uniquely gifted. The Bible is clear about this:

> For you created my inmost being;
> you knit me together in my mother's womb.
> I praise you because I am fearfully and wonderfully made;
> your works are wonderful,
> I know that full well.
> My frame was not hidden from you
> when I was made in the secret place.
> When I was woven together in the depths of the earth,
> your eyes saw my unformed body.
> All the days ordained for me were written in your book
> before one of them came to be (Psalm 139:13-16).

> We have different gifts, according to the grace given us
> (Romans 12:6).

Ponder those words. *I am fearfully and wonderfully made...When I was woven together in the depths of the earth, Your eyes saw my unformed body. All the days ordained for me were written in Your book before one of them came to be...We have different gifts, according to the grace given us.*

You are beautiful in God's eyes. Your Creator saw *your* unformed body before you came to be. All *your* days were written in God's book before you even lived your first one! This means that God knew what your strengths would be as well as your weaknesses before you were even an embryo. He knew what skills you'd possess and what you'd be lousy at before you reached your first trimester of life. And He knew what you'd be passionate about and couldn't care less about before you took your first breath. In fact, friend, He's the One who placed all those likes, dislikes, skills, abilities, and passions in you in the first place. He designed you.

And because He designed you, He watches you. He sees the things that you think go unnoticed. He sees you when you give selflessly and you're not in the spotlight. He sees you when you're faithfully tucking your kids in bed late at night. Giving an encouraging word to a friend who is broken. Comforting your sick husband. Cooking dinner for your family religiously every night. Even though you're not recognized with the accolades of the world, God is so pleased with your faithfulness that your plaques are being designed in heaven.

> When you do a charitable deed, do not sound a trumpet before you as the hypocrites do in the synagogues and in the streets, that they may have glory from men…But when you do a charitable deed…[do it] in secret, and your Father who sees in secret will Himself reward you openly (Matthew 6:2-4 NKJV).

Maybe your reward will come through your kids. Maybe through your marriage. Maybe through that special someone who will rise up and call you blessed for His special sake. Regardless of the way, you will be rewarded openly! So keep walking with Him.

Why would God take all the time necessary to craft you in a way that makes you one of a kind if He didn't have plans to use you in a special way?

From a young age, most of us are trained to be humble and not brag. Miss Manners is right—no one wants to be around an egotistical braggart—but in our childhood we often start focusing more on what we *can't* do rather than what we *can* do. When that happens, our beauty is hidden, and our uniqueness gets lost. Unfortunately, many of us don't rediscover our uniqueness until adulthood—and often only after an intense, purposeful, and prolonged search. Tragically, some never find it again.

If you've forgotten how beautiful you are, and if you cannot hear your Father's voice encouraging you and compassionately whispering to you how wonderful and uniquely gifted you really are, now is the time to listen again. Now is the time to rediscover the qualities God placed in you before you came into being. Those are the qualities God wants you to use so you can live His dream for you.

As you begin to focus on what you're good at and what you love to do, you may have to deflect negative self-talk such as this:

- *What makes you think God made you special?*
- *Other people have talents, but God missed you when giving them out.*
- *Focusing on things you're good at will just give you a big ego. Better not to focus on them.*
- *Identifying what you're passionate about won't change anything. You're still stuck in a dead-end job.*

❧ *Not everyone can live a life bigger than what she dreamed. What makes you think God has that in mind for you?*

❧ *You're too _____ (fat, dumb, overeducated, undereducated, selfish) for God to use.*

These are some of the lies we tell ourselves and society tells us—often to keep us in our place. But where is our place? I believe it's where God has called and created us to be. Many of us have allowed these lies to keep us where we are. We haven't dared to dream that God placed our unique skills and abilities in us in order to help us take our rightful place in the plan He created especially for us.

If you're one of the lucky ones and are already living God's dream for your life, be thankful. And pledge to encourage a friend to keep looking for her own God-designed niche. If you're floundering and frustrated in your search for God's plan for your life, consider that though His dream for you is likely bigger than you imagine, He may use you in small ways to live it. The humble skill of being a good listener may, in fact, save someone else's life. Your gentle touch may offer hope to one who is ill. Your willingness to forgive a friend may be the catalyst that starts her on the path to self-forgiveness. The hug you shared with a neighbor last week may have been just enough to encourage her to continue to work on her marriage rather than to give up on it.

In other words, though God's plan for you is big, you may be called to live it out in small, seemingly *un*extraordinary ways, using skills and abilities you don't think are all that special or unique. But remember, this is God's economy we're talking about, not ours.

The skills we're called to use may not be extraordinary. But the way we use them can lead to surprising results. Only when you truly know you're created in His image and you see yourself as beautiful in His eyes can you appreciate and fully assume the gifts He's given you.

In this way we are like the various parts of a human body. Each part gets its meaning from the body as a whole, not the other way around. The body we're talking about is Christ's body of chosen people. Each of us finds our meaning and function as a part of his body. But as a chopped-off finger or cut-off toe we wouldn't amount to much, would we? So since we find ourselves fashioned into all these excellently formed and marvelously functioning parts in Christ's body, let's just go ahead and be what we were made to be, without enviously or pridefully comparing ourselves with each other, or trying to be something we aren't.

If you preach, just preach God's Message, nothing else; if you help, just help, don't take over; if you teach, stick to your teaching; if you give encouraging guidance, be careful that you don't get bossy; if you're put in charge, don't manipulate; if you're called to give aid to people in distress, keep your eyes open and be quick to respond; if you work with the disadvantaged, don't let yourself get irritated with them or depressed by them. Keep a smile on your face (Romans 12:4-8 MSG).

Each of the skills (also known as gifts) referred to in Romans 12 are pretty ordinary: teaching, encouraging, and leading. The way you use these skills makes them unique.

If you haven't already found your gifts and decided how to use them, now is the time.

Live the
DREAM

To capture God's dream for your life, you must recognize and know how to use the special gifts God has blessed you with.

JOURNAL
PROMPT

❖ What are your spiritual gifts?

❖ How have you used your spiritual gifts to honor God in the past month?

❖ What little skill do you have that God can use for big things?

Day 4

Focus on Your Strengths

Always be a first-rate version of yourself, instead
of a second-rate version of somebody else.
Judy Garland

In his bestselling book *The Purpose-Driven Life,* Rick Warren writes, "God will never ask you to dedicate your life to a task you have no talent for. On the other hand, the abilities you *do* have are a strong indication of what God wants you to do with your life."[1]

So, sister, what are you good at?

Most of us spend far more time focusing on what we're *not* good at rather than what we *are* good at. But human resource professionals tell us that the greatest opportunities for personal growth and development come from focusing on our strengths, not our weaknesses. This is counter to the message corporate America habitually sends to its employees. In job evaluations, managers often spend more time pointing out employee weaknesses than building on strengths. And when setting goals, managers frequently ask employees to become better at what they are not naturally good at rather than asking them to focus on their strengths and capitalize on them for the benefit of the company.

We all have a choice. We can focus on what we're *not* good at, or we can focus on what we *are* good at. Extraordinary women focus on what they are good at and use their gifts to further God's kingdom.

Extraordinary women also use their strengths in little things to make a big difference.

Mother Teresa knew that caring for the sick and poor one person at a time would make a big difference for each person she cared for. She didn't know that her compassion would make a big impression on the larger world as well.

You may not have heard of Genevieve Piturro. She was heartbroken as a volunteer at children's shelters when she realized that the kids slept in the same clothes they'd worn all day. Remembering the warm comfort of her own pajamas as a child, Piturro started purchasing PJs and taking them to children's centers. In 2001, when the demand for pajamas grew beyond her own ability to meet it, she started the Pajama Program. Since then, more than 10,000 pairs of pajamas and over 8000 books have found children to wear and read them—and thousands of children have learned that though they are parentless or in difficult circumstances, someone still cares. (To learn more or to donate to the Pajama Program, visit www.pajamaprogram.org.)

When Kim Newlen left her teaching job to stay home with her daughter, she experienced loneliness. Instead of wallowing in it, she decided to do something about it. She created a monthly gathering for women that didn't require them to send an RSVP or extend a reciprocal invitation. The gatherings, called Sweet Monday, offer brief spiritual encouragement, food, and most importantly, fun! Ten years after the first group met, Sweet Mondays are providing even more opportunities for fellowship as women across the country have adapted the idea. Because of this ministry, many women who stopped going to church have returned, and others who did not know Christ have made a commitment to Him. Kim, the lonely mom, has now turned into an encourager extraordinaire and has written *Sweet Monday: Women's Socials on a Shoestring*. (You can learn more about Sweet Monday at www.sweetmonday.com.)

Each of these women began her journey by meeting her own needs and the needs of others. God took it from there in ways that they could not anticipate.

One of my strengths is that I'm organized. I always have a plan and can handle details and deadlines. When I'm going somewhere, I have a complete itinerary (and usually printed directions from MapQuest!). I live by lists and read the directions when I'm doing something I've never done before. And then I actually follow them. This drives my husband, Tim, crazy.

I can either focus on my strengths and use them for service to God and others, or I can berate myself for my weaknesses. The first option is positive and empowering. The second option would simply make me feel bad about myself and not help me accomplish anything—except feeling bad.

Most of us can easily come up with a list of weaknesses. But can you easily articulate your strengths as well? If not, take a look at the following list and circle or highlight any of the words that describe your strengths:

flexible	motivating	risk taker
supportive	systematic	analyzer
intuitive	assertive	outgoing
sensitive	deliberate	confident
generous	cooperative	decisive
loyal	patient	diplomatic
enthusiastic	influential	optimistic
organized	visionary	problem solver
reliable	determined	results oriented
peacemaker	questioner	team player
fact finder	orderly	cautious

This list isn't all-inclusive, but it's a good place to start identifying and verbalizing your strengths. Once you're able to do that, you're ready to move to the next step, which is to make a specific list of ways you can use these strengths.

> God's various gifts are handed out everywhere; but they all originate in God's Spirit. God's various ministries are carried out everywhere; but they all originate in God's Spirit. God's various expressions of power are in action everywhere; but God himself is behind it all. Each person is given something to do that shows who God is (1 Corinthians 12:4-6 MSG).

Mother Teresa used the gift of extending mercy to the poor and sick. Genevieve Piturro used the gift of contributing pajamas to children. And Kim Newlen used the gift of connecting women in her living room.

What have you been given to do that shows who God is? Serve on the governing board at your church? Help at your local food pantry? Organize a fundraiser to support missionaries? Handle the finances of a charity? Teach Sunday school? Attend Sunday school? Help build sets for the annual Christmas drama at your church? Lead a music team? Make hospital visits? Provide transportation to and from church for those who can't drive? The possibilities are endless.

Here's what else is endless: God's ability to reach down from heaven and show Himself to other people through you. You are Christ on earth every day to the people around you. And when you focus on using your strengths to show Christ and refuse to wallow in your weaknesses, your light will shine brighter and your reach will extend further than you ever imagined.

Live the
DREAM

*Choose to focus on what you are good at and use
your gifts to further God's kingdom.*

JOURNAL
PROMPTS

- What are your three biggest strengths?
- How can you best reveal God's glory and handiwork through the abilities He's given you?
- What gifts and abilities do you have that you can use to benefit your small group, family, coworkers, church, or community organization?

Day 5

Ages, Stages, and Changes

Be willing to be uncomfortable.
Be comfortable being uncomfortable. It may get tough,
but it's a small price to pay for living a dream.
PETER McWILLIAMS

The Bible clearly teaches that we all will journey through various seasons in life. Read Ecclesiastes 3:1-8:

> There is a time for everything
> and a season for every activity under heaven:
> a time to be born and a time to die,
> a time to plant and a time to uproot,
> a time to kill and a time to heal,
> a time to tear down and a time to build,
> a time to weep and a time to laugh,
> a time to mourn and a time to dance,
> a time to scatter stones and a time to gather them,
> a time to embrace and a time to refrain,
> a time to search and a time to give up,
> a time to keep and a time to throw away,
> a time to tear and a time to mend,
> a time to be silent and a time to speak,
> a time to love and a time to hate,
> a time for war and a time for peace.

Maybe you're reading this book and thinking, *God may have had a dream for me, but I missed it.* Or *I'm too far along in life for God to be able to use me.* Or *God might want to use me, but my life is a mess right now!*

Regardless of what your circumstances are, what your background is, how much money you have, or what your skills are, God is looking for a willing heart. And that's something you can develop—even if you're not quite ready to commit at this point. God is ready whenever you are.

Extraordinary women know that God can use them at all the ages and stages and in all the changes of life.

I consider my mother an extraordinary woman. I know that I'm biased, but I've seen how her willing heart has enabled God to use her for something she never imagined after an unexpected stage of life was thrust upon her, forcing unwanted change.

My father was 59 years young when he was diagnosed with bone marrow cancer. My mother was just 58. They had been married for 40 years when his diagnosis changed their discussions from talk of retirement and moving closer to their grandchildren to discussions about doctor appointments and treatment options.

As a family, we prayed fervently for healing. My mom became my dad's nurse, and though her heart was breaking, she remained strong for him. She kept track of his medicines and served as his caregiver through his bone marrow transplant. She helped him handle his business affairs and took over the family finances. She coordinated his schedule, and when keeping it became too difficult, she insisted he lighten his load. Finally, when we realized my father would not be healed in this life, my mom gave my dad the precious gift of discussing what would happen to her after his death and letting him help her make plans. He even made sure my mom had a house built near us so we would be close to her after his passing.

Though dealing with her own sadness, my mom has done a remarkable job of responding to the unexpected change of becoming a widow much earlier than she ever dreamed. More importantly, she realizes she's in a new stage. And that's where her willing heart comes in.

Rather than allowing herself to be defined by a single word—"widow"—my mom realizes that she can help others because of the new stage she's in. She not only continues to be a great support to my sister and me and our families but also ministers to others who have lost spouses. Though my mom is not a widow by choice, she allows God to use her to help others through the grieving process. Watching God use her has been enlightening to me, and I often wonder how and where He'll use me as I also travel through the ages, stages, and changes that are ahead for me—ones that only He knows about.

Even though I don't understand why God didn't heal my father, I know that God loves me, and I choose to continue to believe in Him and His promises. God is good in all ages, stages, and changes. I may never fully understand why things happen the way they do, but I continue to put my trust in God. Doing so is the first step to having a willing heart. And having a willing heart is the secret to living God's dream for you.

Live the
DREAM

God can and will use you in all the ages, stages, and changes of life.

JOURNAL
PROMPTS

- ✿ What age, stage, or change have you recently experienced (wanted or unwanted)? Brainstorm ways God could possibly use you as a result.

- ✿ The Bible tells us, "There is a time for everything and a season for every activity under heaven." Does this knowledge help you to be patient for God to reveal His plan for you?

- ✿ Make a timeline of the past 20 years of your life. Fill it in with significant happenings (both good and bad) as well as key people who impacted your life throughout the years. Compare it to where you are today. Do you see why God brought certain people into your life when He did? Can you get a sense for what God was teaching you during the triumphs and tragedies of the past 20 years and why He intervened when He did?

Week 2

Secrets to Knowing God Really Loves You

Though our feelings come and go,
God's love for us does not.
C.S. LEWIS

At age four, all little girls love their daddies. I remember our daughter, Megan, dancing on Tim's feet as a little girl. She looked up at him with dazzled eyes and a glowing smile. She knew she was the apple of his eye and basked in that assurance. She still does.

Becca's story is a little different. Like most little girls, she always waited for her daddy to make that last turn and come up the driveway each night. One evening, with her nose pressed up against the windowpane and condensation forming on the window from every breath she took, she waited. And waited. But no dad—he never came. She never saw him again, and she dealt with his abandonment for the rest of her life.

An absent father is an unfortunate reality that cuts into the heart of a child more deeply than we tend to realize. Nearly 40 percent of America's children will wake up in a home tomorrow where their biological fathers don't live. Even more troubling, nearly half of those kids haven't seen their dads in the past 12 months.

And one question pierces the hearts of all these children, especially little girls: *Do you really love me, Daddy?* Knowing whether or not your dad really loves you is difficult if you don't know him or struggle a lot in your relationship with him. Whether they realize it or not, many women spend their whole lives seeking the answer to this most critical life question. Some never find it. They never break free.

The same is often true with our heavenly Father, whom we can't physically see or touch. Too often our experience with God mirrors the relationship we have—or don't have—with our earthly fathers. But the two really have no connection. To fully embrace God's love, we must first understand how much God really loves us—regardless of the status of our relationship with our earthly fathers.

In this chapter, you'll discover how to find God's love for you, and you'll find assurance that nothing can keep you from the everlasting love He has to offer.

Day 1

Chased

I'm just a girl standing in front of a boy, asking him to love her.
Anna Scott (Julia Roberts) in *Notting Hill*

Did you play tag when you were a little girl? I did.

Nestled in the plains of northeastern Montana was a small church my grandfather had planted years earlier. Each week my sister and I and all the other kids in the church were anxious for the Sunday school bell to ring. It meant we had 20 minutes to play together before the church service officially began. Tag was the game of choice, and most of the time the boys were "it." I never figured out why, but even if a boy tagged me, he remained "it" until all the girls were tagged. I loved being chased by the boys around the churchyard. It was innocent and fun. Then we grew up, and it became even more exciting.

How did you feel when your husband, fiancé, or boyfriend began chasing you? You remember, I'm sure. Waiting by the phone for him to call. Being surprised by a bouquet of flowers or a box of candies. Noticing the way he looked at you and wondering when the next date would be or what adventure he had planned next. Feeling the warmth of his lips on yours. Knowing that you were the only one he wanted to chase, that to him, nobody else in the world was more beautiful than you. Regardless of your age, when you're chased, the little-girl, giggly feeling resonates.

We all want to be chased. When we are, we relax. We feel beautiful and free.

In their book *Captivating,* John and Stasi Eldredge describe a woman who feels loved and sought after:

> We have all heard it said that a woman is most beautiful when she is in love. It's true. When a woman knows that she is loved and loved deeply, she glows from the inside. This radiance stems from a heart that has had its deepest questions answered. "Am I lovely? Am I worth fighting for? Have I been and will I continue to be romanced?" God wants us to be captivated by His beauty.[1]

God loves you. And because He does, He is chasing you—yes *you,* even now.

You might struggle to believe that even with so many people and so many problems in the world, God still has time to pursue you, but He does.

Let yourself be caught. His love is like no other.

Receiving it is a choice. You can begin by saying, *Yes, Lord, I believe.*

Maintaining intimacy with God is also a choice. In today's world, so much tears at a woman's heart and competes for her affections. You can unknowingly, unintentionally, and so subtly give your heart to other things. You've got to want Him with everything you have! But the Bible promises, "When you come looking for me, you'll find me. Yes, when you get serious about finding me and want it more than anything else, I'll make sure you won't be disappointed" (Jeremiah 29:13 MSG). Or as the New King James Version says, "And you will seek Me and find Me, when you search for Me with all your heart."

Referring to seeking God's beauty, Stasi Eldredge continues, "It is rich. It is good. And it is opposed. To pursue intimacy with Christ, you will have to fight for it."

Why do you have to fight for it? Because evil hates God's beauty in you, that's why.

In his book *Turn Your Life Around,* my husband, Tim, refers to this as the path of "disordered affections," which occur when we rely on things other than God to fill the hole in our hearts. Our affections are disordered when everything in life seems crazy, nothing is in sync, priorities are chaotic, and life is overwhelming. Husband. Kids. Work. Family. In-laws. Vacations. Finances. Church. Laundry. Dinner. The pressures of life begin to take away your affection for God. As a result you spend less time with Him. The less time you have with Him, the less beautiful you feel. And the next thing you know, you no longer feel loved.

Do you see what happens? Idolatry takes hold as we turn to other things rather than our Father to calm and soothe our pain—the emptiness or brokenness in our hearts. Tim defines idolatry as "the fruitless pursuit of anything besides God to fill what only He can fill." Shopping. Food. Bad relationships. Breaking free of idolatry requires discipline and holding on to what Paul believed: "Who shall separate us from the love of Christ?...For I am persuaded that neither death nor life, nor angels nor principalities nor powers, nor things present nor things to come, nor height nor depth, nor any other created thing, shall be able to separate us from the love of God which is in Christ Jesus our Lord" (Romans 8:35,38-39 NKJV).

Daily I have to make a decision to choose to be captured and recaptured by God's love.

Rest assured that God actively pursues you. Instead of running, however, allow yourself to be caught. *Ask* to be captured.

> When we finally let go we feel lighter than air. We are once again five-year-olds waiting with anticipation to leap off the steps into open arms with a joyful shout and loud laughter, saying, "Daddy, catch me!"
>
> Something beautiful happens in your soul when you finally *believe* that God's heart is toward you—no matter what. He is the Dad who doesn't want you to go anywhere else but into His arms. He is saying, "Come to Me. I am not going to fail you. I want to show you a way to a better life." He's been waiting for you.[2]

Every day, the Creator of the universe, the Most High God, the Giver of Life pursues you. He longs to love you.

Stop running. Let yourself be captured. Let yourself be loved. Let your life begin anew, and rediscover the little-girl, giggly feeling you so deserve.

Live the
DREAM

God is the Lover of your soul and actively chases you.

JOURNAL
PROMPTS

- ⚜ What do the words "captured by God's love" mean to you? Do they generate a mental image of servitude or a more romantic picture of being pursued by someone who's in love with you?

- ⚜ Does the idea of being captured by God's love have a positive or negative connotation for you?

- ⚜ What do you naturally turn your affections to when you're under stress or duress? How can you rediscover your affection for God?

Day 2

He Loves Me, He Loves Me Not

*To the world you may be one person,
but to one person you may be the world.*
BILL WILSON

I was sitting with my daughter, Megan, as she read through this chapter's outline. When she read the title "He Loves Me, He Loves Me Not," she giggled comically.

"What's so funny over there?" Tim asked, watching TV from the sofa nearby. He had just asked me if I used to play that game with daisies when I was little.

Megan responded playfully, "When I was a little girl, I remember plucking the petals off the daisies and saying 'He loves me, He loves me not' in the landscape outside the house. And the funny thing is, I wasn't even interested in boys yet."

That's when I protested, "What do you mean, *yet?*"

As her mother, I may have been slightly overprotective, but this illustration points to something written deep in the heart of every woman—the longing to be loved. Even before Megan was interested in boys, her heart's desire was to be loved. Like me and you, she will feel this longing a lot more in this life.

Why do we always hope that the last petal we pick is engraved with those three comforting words "he loves me"? Is it simply that we were made for love? Or perhaps that we fear being unloved?

Living in such a confusing world, we can easily miss how beautiful we are to God and how much He really does love us. But extraordinary women long for the love of God and are able to receive it.

Here's what we know: Women are twice as likely as men to suffer from depression, and 20 percent of women can expect to suffer from clinical depression at some time in their lives. At least 33 percent of women have been physically abused, forced into sex, or otherwise abused during their lifetime, and 25 percent of women in North America were molested in childhood.[3]

The open and unhealed wounds plaguing the hearts of women, adding turmoil and stress to everyday life and interpersonal relationships, are huge. Both single women determined to find a life partner and married women frustrated with theirs experience the tension of living with longings unfulfilled.

How do we cope with the tension of feeling unloved? We actively search for love and reach out to find it. Psychologist Ernest Becker wrote that "modern man is drinking and drugging himself out of awareness, or he spends his time shopping, which is the same thing."[4] Statistics reveal that today women control 80 percent of household spending, a market worth $3.25 trillion. And the average debt for a woman with a credit card exceeds $2300.[5] The unbridled anxiety, depression, divorce, and escapism through drugs, alcohol, consumerism, sex, violence, and suicide have suffocated women from the spiritual fresh air of God's love they long for and so desperately need. Dallas Willard alluded to this in his book on spiritual disciplines, stating, "Obviously, the problem is a spiritual one. And so must be the cure."[6]

Evil hates God's beauty in you and is trying to get you to believe God doesn't care about you or doesn't love you. Evil wants you to believe that you mean nothing to Him. But here is the truth: "If anyone acknowledges that Jesus is the Son of God, God lives in him and he in God. And so we know and rely on the love God has for us. God is love. Whoever lives in love lives in God, and God in him" (1 John 4:15-16).

Your ability to understand, accept, and embrace the fact that God loves you is at the heart of finding your freedom. When you accept His love, you can more easily pass it along. His love shines through you.

But first you have to dispel the evil lies running rampant in your mind and accept that God really loves you. There's a simple way to find out if it's true—ask.

An old adage says, "Don't ask if you don't want to know the answer." But the opposite is also true. If you want to know the answer, ask.

When you ask God if He loves you, He will answer because God *is* love. And because He *is* love, everything He does is infused with love.

That's why you long to be certain of God's love for you. Joyce Meyer agrees:

> A confident woman knows that she is loved. She does not fear being unloved, because she knows first and foremost that God loves her unconditionally. To be whole and complete, we need to know that we are loved. Receiving the free gift of God's unconditional love is the beginning of our healing, and the foundation for our new life in Christ.[7]

Being secure in God's love for us is an essential element of handling whatever comes our way. Wife, mother, and grandmother Cathy Hendrick experienced the unimaginable but was able to move through it by holding fast to God's love. On October 24, 2004, her husband and 22-year-old twin daughters were killed in an airplane crash. Following the accident, she asked herself, *Did God love me any less on October twenty-third than He did on October twenty-fourth?* She knew the answer: *No, He did not.*

Says Cathy, "I know He loves me, and of this I am confident. My assurance of His love began many years before the crash. But during these times of brokenheartedness, sickness, and losses, we discover what we really believe about Him and whether we truly put our faith and trust in Him."

By putting her faith in God, Cathy has been able to move through tragedy with her faith intact.

Evil tells you that love can't be trusted. But God will *show* you it can.

God's love shows in the gentle hug of a friend who knows you're hurting but doesn't need to know why. In the flowers delivered on your birthday or the card or e-mail that arrives for no other reason than to cheer you. In your husband's voice when he asks, "How can I help?" and your child's when she says, "You're the best mommy ever." His love shows through the touch of a nurse who inserts the needle into your chemotherapy port and in the mind of the doctor who studies overtime to make sure your treatment is effective. It shows in the act of a neighbor who returns your trash can after it has blown down the street, in the smile of the elderly man who opens the door for you when your arms are full, in the funeral director who gently helps you plan a memorial service befitting your father, and in the neighbor who recognizes you're weary and offers to watch your kids for the afternoon.

"There is no room in love for fear. Well-formed love banishes fear. Since fear is crippling, a fearful life…is one not yet fully formed in love" (1 John 4:18 MSG).

Consider what Meister Eckhart, one of the great Christian mystics, penned in the fourteenth century: "The soul must long for God in order to be set aflame by God's love; but if the soul cannot yet feel this longing, then it must long for the longing. To long for the longing is also from God."

Because God loves us, He puts that longing to be loved—and the longing for Him—in our hearts. No wonder we want that last petal to say, "He loves me."

Live the
DREAM

Long for the love of God and prepare to receive it.

JOURNAL
PROMPTS

- What would you like to ask God about His relationship with you?
- If you're uncomfortable with the idea of asking God if He loves you, take a minute to consider why. Are you afraid the answer will be no? Or that you won't hear any answer at all?
- What are your fears when you think of loving or being loved by another?
- What steps will you begin taking to overcome your fears of being loved?

Day 3

Praise Him in the Storm

Love always involves responsibility, and love always involves sacrifice. And we do not really love Christ unless we are prepared to face His task and to take up His Cross.

WILLIAM BARCLAY

Getaways. Some time off. A break. We all need them, and our bodies usually tell us when it's time.

For one Chicago couple, it was time. Having just buried their son and then lost their entire real estate business in a massive fire, the mom and dad needed to get away with their four daughters. The destination: England.

As the family prepared to leave, the father was called to stay on urgent business. Assuring his wife and four daughters that he would meet up with them a few days later in England, he sent them off together ahead of him. As they sailed away from the New York port, all was well. Hours into their journey, in the middle of the cold Atlantic Ocean, something changed. Another ship appeared from nowhere. *Bang!* People were screaming, yelling, and running frantically. Within 12 minutes of the impact, the ship had sunk beneath the ocean's surface.

Tragedy, heartache, and loss—not one of us is immune to times of trouble. Nobody can escape them. The storms of life are inevitable. Life has its way of handing us many blows. And when storms hit, we can feel forsaken and unloved.

Even Jesus was tempted to feel this way. Hanging on the cross, He cried out, "My God, My God, why have You forsaken me?" (Matthew 27:46 NKJV).

Growing up in a Christian home, I was fortunate enough to hear about and experience God's love from the time I was young. Yet even with that strong foundation, God's love has sometimes seemed elusive to me, like when Tim and I first got married and discovered that saying "I do" doesn't necessarily mean "happily ever after." (At least the first year anyway!) Or when our son, Zach, suffered febrile seizures, and his asthma had us frequenting the hospital the first two years of his life. Or when my father was dying of cancer or Tim's mother battled diabetes, heart failure, and a stroke.

In the midst of trying circumstances, we sometimes allow worry and anger to cloud God's love. That's why we need to respond to the storms of life with a spirit of faith. Worry keeps us focused on earthly things. Anger, not properly dealt with, keeps us focused on how *we'll* make things right again. In both cases, we're focused on something other than God and His everlasting, unconditional love.

Paul understood what we go through. Five times he received 40 lashes minus one. He was beaten with rods three times and shipwrecked just as many. He was stoned once and spent a night and a day in the open sea. He was in danger from rivers, from bandits, from his own people, and from Gentiles. He was in danger in his own country and from false brothers. He hungered, froze, was naked in public, didn't sleep—and still loved God (2 Corinthians 11:24-27).

Even with a thorn in his flesh, Paul learned that God's grace is sufficient, that His strength is made perfect in weakness (2 Corinthians 12:9).

In David's sorrows, he cried, "I am worn out from groaning; all night long I flood my bed with weeping and drench my couch with tears" (Psalm 6:6). In the same prayer he affirms, "The LORD has heard my cry for mercy; the LORD accepts my prayer" (Psalm 6:9).

Jeremiah witnessed the devastation of Judah and Jerusalem and still understood the love of God: "Because of the *LORD's great love* we are not consumed, for his compassions never fail. They are new every morning; great is your faithfulness" (Lamentations 3:22-23).

The opening story in today's reading is that of Horatio G. Spafford. He received a message that read, "Saved alone." It came from his wife, who miraculously survived the shipwreck and reached England. He had lost all four daughters. As he sailed the Atlantic to meet his wife and longtime friend Dwight L. Moody (who had been preaching in England), Spafford sailed over the wreckage. Following the tragedy he penned these words:

> When peace like a river attendeth my way,
> When sorrows like sea billows roll;
> Whatever my lot, Thou has taught me to say,
> It is well, it is well, with my soul.

> Though Satan should buffet, though trials should come,
> Let this blessed assurance control,
> That Christ has regarded my helpless estate,
> And hath shed His own blood for my soul.

> My sin, oh, the bliss of this glorious thought!
> My sin, not in part but the whole,
> Is nailed to the cross, and I bear it no more,
> Praise the Lord, praise the Lord, O my soul!

> And Lord, haste the day when my faith shall be sight,
> The clouds be rolled back as a scroll;
> The trump shall resound, and the Lord shall descend,
> Even so, it is well with my soul.

The question is not whether we'll have storms, it's what we will do with them when they come. Job didn't understand why he was suffering, but he maintained his trust in God anyway. Our responses to struggles in life define our attitude toward God. We can become bitter, or we can press on in faith, knowing that God will not subject us to more than we can handle.

Have you been bitter about life? Or have you praised Him in the storm?

It's your turn to write a song. What will you sing?

Live the
DREAM

Respond to the storms of life with faith
and praise Him in the storm.

JOURNAL
PROMPTS

- ❧ What storms have you recently encountered? Have you been able to sense God's love in the midst of the storm?
- ❧ How has God rescued you from storms in your life?
- ❧ Write the chorus of a song telling God and others what He has done for you.

Day 4

An Unchanging Love

God is unchanging in His love. He loves you.
He has a plan for your life.
Don't let the newspaper headlines frighten you.
God is still sovereign; He's still on the throne.
BILLY GRAHAM

In the midst of life's most difficult changes, including unemployment, illness, loss, relocation, and retirement, you can be comforted by knowing that God's love doesn't change. He's with you in the unemployment office, in the hospital, and in the moving van. He's with you in the infertility clinic and as you begin to collect Social Security. Actually, He's not just *with* you in these places, He's *in* you in these places. And that's a powerful piece of knowledge.

The next time your circumstances cause you to question whether God has abandoned you, close your eyes, breathe deeply, and ask God, *What do I need to know, do, or think to be able to recognize You in this circumstance?* If the answer doesn't come immediately, keep asking even if you must repeat the question for days, months, or years.

God is in you. His love for you is unchanging. That's all you need to know to be able to move through changing circumstances. Hold fast to this knowledge. Christ is holding fast to you.

Hebrews 13:8 tells us that "Jesus Christ is the same yesterday and today and forever." Because He's the same, we know His love for us doesn't change either.

Isn't that a relief? God loves you. Period. You don't have to earn His love. You don't have to be worthy of it. And nothing you do or have done will keep God from loving you.

What a relief to know that our failings won't keep us, our families, or our friends from the love of Christ. Nothing we can do will change His feelings for us. He even loves those people who don't know Him or love Him back! Unbelievably, Jesus loved the very people who tormented and crucified him. Luke 23:34 quotes Jesus as saying, "Father, forgive them, for they do not know what they are doing."

I can't imagine having the fortitude to extend forgiveness to people while they were killing me. I've often been able to offer forgiveness after an incident, when I later realized the person who hurt me was actually in pain herself and lashed out as a result. But I'm not sure I've ever had the strength to forgive someone the moment he or she injured me. Jesus' ability to forgive while He was being physically and mentally tortured reveals His true character.

Further, Luke tells us that even as He hung in agony on the cross, He was able to respond to one of the men hanging next to him.

> One of the criminals who hung there hurled insults at him: "Aren't you the Christ? Save yourself and us!"
>
> But the other criminal rebuked him. "Don't you fear God," he said, "since you are under the same sentence? We are punished justly, for we are getting what our deeds deserve. But this man has done nothing wrong."
>
> Then he said, "Jesus, remember me when you come into your kingdom."
>
> Jesus answered him, "I tell you the truth, today you will be with me in paradise" (Luke 23:39-43).

Even as He was dying, Christ showed love. Extraordinary women know that this love—His love—is unchanging.

Though He's the same yesterday, today, and forever, accepting His love allows *us* to change for the better. He wants to see you and me mature spiritually. He desires that we get rid of unhealthy habits. He longs for us to take time to read the Bible and learn more about His nature. He hopes that we'll grow in faith so we can be more like Him and love without judgment or expecting anything in return. He invites us to talk to Him more each day, to turn all of our thoughts over to Him. He wants to receive our worship and praise. More than anything, He wants to be our Friend. In John 15:15 He tells us, "I no longer call you servants, because a servant does not know his master's business. Instead, I have called you friends, for everything that I learned from my Father I have made known to you."

Take a minute for personal reflection. Though God's love is unchanging, how do *you* need to change in order to more fully embrace His love and friendship? It's a question worth pondering.

Do you need to accept yourself before you can accept God's love more fully?

Do you need to extend or accept forgiveness (to yourself or others) before you bathe in His love?

Do difficulties in your earthly relationships hinder you from trusting your heavenly Father?

One of the best things about life is that tomorrow doesn't have to be the same as today. You can learn new habits, get rid of unwanted ones, identify what's holding you back, and do something about it.

Though Jesus Christ is unchanging, you can change, and He'll help you. Knowing that God really loves you includes understanding that He wants the best for you and is willing to help you get it.

As you learn about Him, you want to be more like Him. Allow His unchanging love to change you.

Live the
DREAM

Though God's love is unchanging,
He's ready to help us change.

JOURNAL
PROMPTS

⸙ How does your assurance of God's unchanging love affect your relationship with Him?

- ❧ Do you need to accept yourself before you can accept God's love more fully? Do you need to extend or accept forgiveness before you bathe in His love?

- ❧ Do difficulties in your earthly relationships hinder you from trusting in your heavenly Father?

- ❧ Are you comfortable with the idea of Jesus as a Friend? If not, why not?

Day 5

Unlikely Angels

When angels visit us, we do not hear the rustle of wings,
nor feel the feathery touch of the breast of a dove;
but we know their presence by the love they create in our hearts.
AUTHOR UNKNOWN

Do you believe in angels? I do.

A recent Harris poll found that nearly 70 percent of Americans, and 76 percent of women, believe angels exist.[8] In my mind, angels have always been beautiful creatures. They're safe, warm, and protective. They watch over us and our children. Psalm 91:11 (MSG) says, "He ordered his angels to guard you wherever you go. If you stumble, they'll catch you; their job is to keep you from falling." I love that.

To some women, the word "angel" brings back fond memories of when Mom or Dad would call her their "little angel." But most of us probably don't look back on our past and think we were really angelic. We're unlikely angels.

When Liz Curtis Higgs was young, she was anything but an angel. She admits to smoking her first joint on the steps of the Statue of Liberty and looking for meaning in drugs, alcohol, and promiscuity. Traveling from town to town as a radio personality, she once worked with Howard Stern. He did the morning show; she did the afternoons. Her life was so messed up, even Howard Stern shook his head and warned her about her reckless lifestyle!

Then God rescued her. Now, as a Christian writer and speaker, she's presented more than 1500 programs for audiences in all 50 states and in Germany, France, England, South Africa, Canada, Ecuador, Scotland, and Indonesia. She's also an award-winning author who's written 24 books focused on God's life-changing love. More than three million copies are in print.

In *Bad Girls of the Bible,* Liz writes eloquently about the shortcomings of women, including herself, and about the God who loves and accepts them.

- Eve let her appetite get the best of her and ate from the tree that God had expressly forbidden (Genesis 3:6).

- Potiphar's wife tried to seduce Joseph and then falsely accused him of being the aggressor when he refused her advances (Genesis 39:6-18).

- Delilah betrayed Samson by nagging him until he revealed the source of his great strength and then selling the information to his enemies (Judges 16:4-21).

- Rahab, a prostitute, cooperated with the Israelite spies only as a last-ditch effort to keep her and her family from being killed (Joshua 2:8-13).

- The Pharisees brought an adulteress before Jesus, who refused to condemn her or allow anyone to cast a stone as called for in the law (John 8:2-11).

Perhaps as you read the above list you thought your name should be added. If so, go ahead and write the sentence that would follow your name. But don't get stuck there. Remind yourself of the freedom you have in Christ.

Mary Magdalene remembered where her freedom came from. As the host of seven demons, she was a perfect slave to evil. (Seven is considered the perfect number in the Greek language, and of course, demons are evil.) Luke 8:2 refers to her as "Mary (called Magdalene), from whom seven demons had come out." Why would she be identified by the one thing she most wanted to be rid of? Diane Langberg suggests that "Mary's history is the black velvet on which the diamond of Jesus shows most clearly. Remembering her captivity points to the greatness of her freedom. Remembering her darkness highlights her new life and the light she now knows."[9]

In Deuteronomy, the Israelites were repeatedly told to remember where they came from. The principle is the same for us: Remembering our slavery reminds us of the One who has set us free.

"For freedom Christ has set us free," but sadly, many women do not let Him free them. Instead, they "submit again to a yoke of slavery" (Galatians 5:1 ESV). Years after their worst mistakes or foolish decisions, their memories and shame still haunt them. Are you one of these women? That's not what God wants for you! Instead, He wants you to know that "if we confess our sins, he is faithful and just and will forgive us our sins and purify us from all unrighteousness" (1 John 1:9). And "as far as the east is from the west, so far has he removed our transgressions from us" (Psalm 103:12).

Nothing you do disqualifies you from being loved by or used by God.

Who would have thought that God would use Liz Curtis Higgs' testimony in such a powerful way? Her willingness to acknowledge her mistakes and misjudgments has touched countless lives, including mine, and encouraged women worldwide. Mary Magdalene's testimony has and will continue to transcend time to bring women back to the heart of God.

Just as we must avoid the mistake of believing our shortcomings disqualify us from God's love, we must also avoid the mistake of waiting until we're perfect to seek a deeper relationship with Him. We need Him most when our lives are messy and uncertain. Having to admit our untidiness often keeps us from approaching our gracious Savior. Don't wait until the mess is cleaned up to pray. You'll be waiting a very long time! Richard Foster says, "The greatest deterrent to an active prayer life is thinking all needs to be right."

Remember, you are His daughter (Galatians 4:6-7), and He's placed angels, even some unlikely angels, all around you to protect you and see you through the brokenness (Psalm 91:11).

Be free.

Live the
DREAM

God loves you and can use you regardless of anything you've done.

JOURNAL
PROMPTS

-ଙ Have you ever experienced something that caused you to think an angel was near? Describe the event.

-ଙ In what ways has God changed you so that He can use you more effectively in the future?

-ଙ Have you done things that you believe may disqualify you from being used by God? If so, acknowledge them and work to release them. God can use anyone to advance His kingdom.

Week 3

Secrets to Meaningful Relationships

If you love someone, tell them.

God. Work. Friends. Dating. Marriage. Family. Parents. Roommates. Church. Life is all about relationships. Each demands a lot of personal time, energy, and heart, and some can be particularly "high maintenance."

Everything in today's world seems to compete with and tear at our relationships with God and others. Trusting others and feeling safe may be difficult for a variety of reasons. Perhaps you grew up without a dad, came from a divorced family, were abused or hurt by someone you should have been able to trust, fought your way through a bad breakup, or are working crazy hours that prohibit close friendships.

In a world filled with online communication and networking, you'd think we would somehow be better connected and closer. But we're not!

A recent study of 1500 Americans revealed some very sobering results about how we are doing in our relationships. "A quarter of Americans have no one with whom they can discuss personal troubles, more than double the number who were similarly isolated in 1985. Overall, the number of people Americans have in their closest circle of confidants has dropped from around three to about two."[1]

We need each other more, not less. Blogs, instant messaging, Myspace,

Facebook, and text messaging are fun and fast, but each result in more time alone and fewer meaningful, deep conversations with one another. Yet when you look back on your life, all that will really matter is whom you loved and who loved you.

In this chapter, we'll discover what it takes to build and maintain significant relationships.

Day 1

Hurry Sickness

*The most serious sign of hurry sickness is a diminished
capacity to love. Love and hurry are fundamentally incompatible.
Love always takes time, and time is the one thing
hurried people don't have.*
JOHN ORTBERG

Who are the most important people in your life?

Right now every mother knows whether she is close to her children—she just knows it. Every wife knows whether she's close to her husband. And you know whether you're close to God.

When we feel close, life is good. And when we don't, it's the pits. We all know that relationships don't just happen.

"But I just don't have time to keep up with everything and everybody," I constantly hear from women everywhere. And I feel the same way a lot too! Being close takes hard work—feeling safe and free with one another. But we need to be careful. When we are pulled in every direction, we can easily give our hearts to other things and develop disordered affections. Consider this:

- American children ages 2 to 17 watch television an average of 1180 minutes per week. Parents spend 38.5 minutes per week in meaningful conversation with their children.[2]
- Adults and teens will spend nearly five months (3518

hours) next year watching television, surfing the Internet, reading daily newspapers, and listening to personal music devices.[3]

- ≈ The average work year for prime-age working couples has increased by nearly 700 hours in the last two decades, and high levels of emotional exhaustion at the end of the workday are the norm for 25 to 30 percent of the workforce.[4]

- ≈ More than half of all consumers, at all income levels, say that lack of time is a bigger problem than lack of money, according to a survey in the *Yankelovich Monitor*.[5]

The lack of relational time, I believe, is a spiritual problem. If the evil one can't make you bad, he'll make you busy. In order to grow in love for others and love for Christ, we *must* slow down and stay connected to Him and others. I think Mother Teresa understood this as she warned, "Everybody today seems to be in such a terrible rush, anxious for greater developments and greater riches and so on, so that children have very little time for their parents. Parents have very little time for each other, and in the home begins the disruption of peace in the world."

Jesus realized that time was an essential element of meaningful relationships. Though He had many followers, He selected 12 to spend time with, teaching them what they needed to know to help spread the gospel after His death (Mark 6:30-32). He took the time to have dinner with Zacchaeus, a despised tax collector (Luke 19:1-10). He loitered at a well to speak truth to a Samaritan woman—even though Jews were not to associate with Samaritans (John 4:1-26). He spent time away from the crowd communicating privately with God, His Father (Luke 5:16). In each of these examples, Jesus takes the time to invest in other people and in His own relationship with God—the most meaningful relationship of all. We must follow His model.

Maybe a shift in thinking is necessary. Instead of "spending" time with others we would be wise to "invest" our time. Spending leaves less for ourselves. Investing enables us to profit—in our relationship with others and through their relationship with us. Investing time in others is at the core of building meaningful relationships.

We cannot change the number of hours in a day, and we cannot make time go faster or slower. But we can change the way we fill up our time. Ask yourself this: When you sit with others, are you really present with them in your mind?

Jesus took time to connect with those in His path. He gave each of them His undivided attention—a good investment. Unlike me, Jesus didn't run through His day with a planner in one hand and a cell phone in the other. He didn't try to squeeze as many people and activities into the day as possible. Richard Swenson describes Jesus' lifestyle:

> Jesus never seemed to be in a hurry...The Bible never says anything about Him running. Apparently, Jesus believed that very little of lasting spiritual or emotional value happens in the presence of speed. Jesus understood that busyness, productivity, and efficiency are speed words, not kingdom words. At times they are appropriate values—but they are never transcendent. Jesus understood that meditation, wisdom, and worship are slow, mellow, and deep.[6]

Jesus also understood that our willingness to give ourselves to others is what really leads to meaningful connection. Why? Because it builds loyal friendships, trusted family ties, and loving relationships. But loyalty, trust, and love only come when we give ourselves to others—over time.

The biblical characters Jonathan and David understood this. Youthful admiration for one another led to friendship over the years. David and Jonathan's relationship stood the tests of difficult decisions and conflicting loyalties. They fought through the adversity by staying loyal to God and to one another. They built trust and strengthened their relationship. But it all started with Jonathan giving himself to David: "Jonathan, out of his deep love for David, made a covenant with him. He formalized it with solemn gifts: his own royal robe and weapons—armor, sword, bow, and belt" (1 Samuel 18:3-4 MSG).

Jonathan practiced his faithfulness to God in his relationship with David. Integrity, truth, intimacy, and loyalty characterized his side of the friendship. And even though we can never be sure we'll have a friend like Jonathan in our lives, we can be sure we're being a Jonathan to others.

Healthy friendships, marriages, and family ties don't happen overnight. Loyalty, trust, and love take time.

Don't let hurry and the resulting clutter of everyday life rob you of your most precious gift—relationships.

Live the
DREAM

Investing time in others is at the core of building meaningful relationships.

JOURNAL
PROMPTS

- ❦ Brainstorm a list of inexpensive ways you can connect with others.
- ❦ Who haven't you been in contact with for a while that you'd like to make an effort to see or talk to?
- ❦ What are the biggest obstacles that keep you from spending time with people you enjoy being with, and how can you overcome them?

Day 2

Forgiveness

Forgive, and you will be forgiven.
LUKE 6:37

As I prayed with a confused and tired young mother of two, she tearfully told me her tragic story and sobbed, "After all he has done to me and said to me and the way he has treated me, I could never forgive him." Agreeing with her in my spirit, I had to take a deep breath and get control of how I felt toward her husband too.

One thing is sure, I couldn't blame her for those thoughts and feelings. When someone who is supposed to love us intentionally violates or hurts us, making sense of it all and forgiving is difficult. I have often struggled with the whole forgiveness thing. Yet God calls us to do it every day.

Your child is dishonest to you. A friend betrays you. Your boss disrespects you in front of other coworkers. Your man lied and even cheated, breaking the trust you worked so hard to build. The result is often burning anger, resentment, fear, or a pillow drenched in tears night after night. You can feel sick to the stomach as the frustration, stubbornness, and bitterness from being hurt well up inside.

For some, the hurt and personal violation by others cuts so deeply into their being that they face a barrage of unpredictable emotions that they've never felt before. Others become numb and emotionless. If we aren't careful, the pain and anger will give way to resentment and bitterness, becoming a corrosive cancer and eventually destroying us if we won't let go and forgive.

For individuals and relationships to be healthy, forgiveness is essential.

Why? Because forgiveness is always our responsibility. Reconciliation (which is often confused with forgiveness) takes two, the offended and the offender, and it may or may not happen. In cases of abuse and violence, putting things back the way they were may not be safe or prudent. Noted forgiveness research expert Dr. Everett Worthington helps us further understand: "The way of forgiveness is hard. Forgiveness isn't for wimps and wusses. In many ways, the destructive power of unforgiveness is much easier than the tough, steely pull of forgiveness."[7]

Jesus taught us a lot about forgiveness through the life of Peter. When Jesus was on trial, Peter waited outside, cold and damp. The young girl attending the door invited him inside to get warm and asked, "Aren't you a disciple?" He said no.

Later, as he stood around the fire getting warm, one of the men he was standing with asked, "You aren't one of his disciples, are you?" Again, he said no.

Finally a man warming beside him challenged him even more. "Didn't I see you in the garden with him?" For the third and final time, he denied it.

Imagine what Peter felt as he watched Jesus die on the cross at Calvary, knowing he had betrayed the Messiah. Or what Jesus felt knowing one of His own disciples denied Him at the same time that the rest of the world was against Him. Yet Jesus, raised from the dead, came to Peter and forgave him.

Jesus challenges us to do the same with those who hurt us. He says, "If he sins against you seven times in a day, and seven times comes back to you and says, 'I repent,' forgive him" (Luke 17:4).

Why must we forgive?

First, because we're called to it. True biblical forgiveness involves applying the grace and forgiveness we receive from Christ to those who've hurt us. For relationships to succeed, they must be built on the capacity to forgive. Healthy relationships know it well.

Second, forgiveness frees both the unforgiven and the unforgiving (Matthew 6:14-15; 18:32-33; Ephesians 4:31-32; Colossians 3:12-13). Though trust and confidence may take time, when we genuinely seek out and act upon forgiveness, we allow for healing and provide the foundation for reconciliation in the relationship. Just as our Father gives freely (1 John 1:9), we should too.

I often hear women say, "Julie, if I forgive him, I'm just excusing his behavior." Don't get me wrong: Forgiveness never excuses or tolerates continued sinful or cruel behaviors. Neither does it mean turning your head and ignoring the offense. Rather, by extending forgiveness, you choose not to keep score, get even, or evaluate the sincerity of the request.

When you forgive, you grow in love. You build trust. And you create opportunities for healing and intimacy.

Healthy relationships demand forgiveness. The *why* may seem easy to understand; the *how* part is what we have trouble figuring out.

Dr. Everett Worthington has laid out a pyramid, mapping the process of forgiveness. I will briefly outline it here. (For a more detailed look into the process, I encourage you to look for his book *Five Steps to Forgiveness: The Art and Science of Forgiving*.)

The first step to forgiveness is recalling the hurt rather than denying anything ever happened. (By the way, denial is sometimes the easier thing to do.) This doesn't mean you dwell on being a victim or blame and badger the one who hurt you. It just simply means you recognize that you were wronged.

Once you name the hurt done to you, attempt to empathize with the one who hurt you. This is difficult, but try to put yourself in his or her shoes. This helps you understand the human condition and the stressors on the other person that may have led him or her to hurt you in the first place. Imagine Jesus trying to understand why Peter betrayed Him and the pressure Peter was feeling at the time.

As you begin to identify with the transgressor, offer the altruistic gift of forgiveness. As Worthington writes, "Have you ever harmed or offended a friend, parent, or partner who later forgave you? Think about your guilt. Then consider the way you felt when you were forgiven. When you think long and hard about this, you might be willing to be selfless and give the gift of forgiveness to those who have hurt you."[8]

Once you've forgiven the transgressor, tell him or her. When you do, you are less likely to question your decision later.

Finally, hold on to the forgiveness. When uncertainty arises, find ways to prevent the anger, bitterness, and resentment from settling in again (Hebrews 12:15). Accepting a sincere apology means you will not continuously bring up past behavior and demand multiple apologies. Honor yourself, your relationships, and those you love by attempting to put forgiven behaviors behind you while resolving to build a stronger future for the relationship.

Forgiveness involves setting aside the offense and never using it as a weapon against the other person. At the heart, forgiveness is about grace. When God forgives us, He sets aside our punishment. He is the source of our forgiveness (Ephesians 4:32). Because He forgives, we can forgive.

Live the
DREAM

Forgiveness is essential to loving and being loved.

JOURNAL
PROMPTS

- ❧ Have you yet to forgive someone? Are you harboring bitterness in your heart because of unforgiveness? What can you do to resolve it?
- ❧ Do you need to seek forgiveness from others? If so, what steps do you need to take?
- ❧ How have you responded to the forgiveness God has granted you on a daily basis? Do you take His grace for granted?

Day 3

Can You Hear Me Now?

The greatest communication tool God created is your ears.
KEN DAVIS

We Clintons seem to have a million things in our home that distract us. We're often blitzed with several conversations and things going on at the same time. Phones ring, text messages arrive, TV shows blare...and when we have a meal together, someone in the house wants *SportsCenter* on in the background! I'll bet your life is the same.

With so much going on, miscommunication often occurs. One time, Tim stood in the foyer of a crowded restaurant watching the lunch crowd pour in—looking all over for me. He couldn't find me. I was at a restaurant several miles away, standing in the foyer and looking for him. We had planned lunch the night before and discussed it again that morning. But somehow we blew it. Fortunately, a phone call solved the problem.

Miscommunicating lunch plans is a minor incident. But how often during serious discussions or heartfelt talks do couples completely ignore or half-listen to each other? Quite often. In fact, up to 90 percent of couples seeking counseling say communication and "talk" issues are at the root of their problems. In his book *Margin,* Richard Swenson notes that most couples spend an average of only four minutes a day in meaningful conversation. As a nation, we are distracted and disconnected. Yet nothing holds more potential for enriching intimacy and connectedness than effective and encouraging communication.

Scripture is pretty clear on this. "Be quick to listen, slow to speak and slow to become angry" (James 1:19). Also, answering a matter before it's fully heard and understood is foolish and shameful (Proverbs 18:13).

I've heard people say that God gave us two ears and only one mouth for a purpose: to listen twice as much as we talk. I bet if we paid attention, however, we'd discover that most of us talk at least twice as much (if not more) than we listen.

Communication involves both sending and receiving messages. Of these two, truly listening to the message you're receiving may be the most important.

Listening is an essential part of building meaningful relationships. The better we are able to listen, the easier we can identify potential problems and areas of pain and miscommunication before they become problems.

In order to be heard, you've got to hear, even when your husband is cold or indifferent, your kids are yanking on your shirt, or your friend calls you seeking advice late at night when you're tired. When others are talking, we need to be quick to turn around, pay attention, and listen.

I wonder about my own listening skills. Do I listen as closely as I can? Do I sometimes pretend I'm listening when I'm really not? Do I listen without really hearing? Do I make sure the environment is such that I can listen carefully when someone is baring their soul to me?

Have you sometimes felt as if someone wasn't listening to you? Can you remember feeling hurt, frustrated, angry, and unimportant? Have you ever wondered how many times you've unknowingly made others feel the same way? Have you confused not talking for listening? I know I have. The truth is that occasionally, when my lips are closed and I should be listening, my ears are also closed or my mind is wandering. Not intentionally—it just happens. I get distracted.

I'm tired of distractions though. I want to listen the way God does. "This is the confidence we have in approaching God: that if we ask anything according to His will, He hears us" (1 John 5:14). When others approach me, I want them to have the confidence that I hear them.

As I write, I realize this means turning off my cell phone and the TV occasionally. It means halting my multitasking and making eye contact with my children, even when dinner is late or the laundry needs folding. It means inviting a colleague to my office to talk privately rather than solving problems when passing in the hallway, even though that's sometimes easiest. It means arranging for one-on-one time with my spouse, my children, my mother, my sister, and my girlfriends, even though I feel crunched for time.

How do we relate with others in such a way as to find love?

- Be a good listener (James 1:19).
- Reflect and think through what is being spoken (Proverbs 15:23).
- Be sensitive to and respectful of your partner (Ephesians 4:31; 1 Peter 3:7).
- Speak the truth—but always in love (Ephesians 4:15; Colossians 3:9).
- Don't fight or respond in anger (Proverbs 17:14; 18:7; Ephesians 4:26; 1 Peter 3:9).
- Confess and forgive when necessary (Proverbs 17:9; Ephesians 4:32; James 5:16).

Other people aren't the only ones I need to listen to. Above all, I must listen to God. I long to hear His voice in my heart. When I hear it, I'm more able to be sensitive to the needs of those around me and more able to listen and really hear what they are saying. When I hear His voice, I'm more confident about the decisions I must make and the actions I must take. When I hear His voice, I can rest easy, knowing I'm wrapped in His love (Jeremiah 31:3).

Please open the eyes of my heart, Lord, so that I can clearly hear You. And as You do that, please open my ears so that I might truly hear those around me, for I know that the prescription for love (listening) is easy. Filling it is hard.

When you fill the listening prescription, you'll feel connected to those who love you.

Live the
DREAM

Listening is the means to learning and understanding,
and it's in learning and understanding that we find love.

JOURNAL
PROMPTS

ꝏ Who do you need to really listen to today?

ꝏ Do you consider yourself an excellent listener, a fair listener, or a poor listener?

ꝏ Who in your life really listens to you, and what can you learn from their listening skills?

Day 4

Pain Hurts...and Helps

God whispers to us in our pleasures, speaks to us in our conscience,
but shouts in our pains: It is His megaphone to rouse a deaf world.
C.S. Lewis

He was oblivious. Perhaps blind. But it happened.

As a 22-year-old soldier, Bill Wilson accepted his first drink. When he welcomed alcohol into his life that day, he didn't think about his deadbeat alcoholic father or his carefree mother, who both left him in Vermont when he was just ten years old. His father went to Canada and his mother to Boston. The predisposition to alcoholism went unrecognized.

And it was easy to see why. Working his way through the ranks, he became a second lieutenant in the military and later found corporate and financial success as a stockbroker in New York City. Bill Wilson was a natural leader and a hard worker, and in 1918 he became a married man. The lucky girl was Lois Burnham.

Together, by motorcycle, they traveled the country. They were young, vivacious, and living on the adrenaline of his business success. Life was good.[9]

But it didn't last long. Life's celebration quickly turned into a destructive, damning plight. Alcohol was no longer just a celebratory bliss; it also became a toxic mask for Bill's depression. He began to show up at work hungover and to verbally offend clients and coworkers. In those days of prohibition, he hid in underground speakeasies for days at a time, leaving Lois to love him back to sobriety. When the stock market crashed in 1929, Bill crashed with it, losing both his job and apartment. Left with nothing, he and Lois moved into her father's home.

Most of us can relate to Bill's condition, either through our own personal experience or by knowing somebody who's been there. Such stories are not uncommon. We all have problems and pain in life. What we do with the problems and pain will differentiate the heroes from the common man. Some people fight through the pain, and others submit to its devastating effects.

For Bill Wilson, the end had come—not to his marriage, his health, or his life, but to his tolerance of alcohol. Bill's fourth admission to the hospital was finally the crisis he needed. He hit rock bottom, and when he did, he reached out to the God he had never known, realizing for the first time that the only thing that could save him from dying of alcoholism was his newfound faith and fellowship.

Bill cofounded Alcoholics Anonymous after meeting a fellow alcoholic named Dr. Bob Smith, a surgeon from Akron, Ohio. In its first four years the movement produced 100 sober alcoholics, and today more than 2 million people call themselves members.

God often uses the most painful parts of our lives to heal others and bring them to Him. He is the "God of all healing counsel...[who] comes alongside us when we go through hard times, and before you know it, he brings us alongside someone else who is going through hard times so that we can be there for that person just as God was there for us" (2 Corinthians 1:3-5 MSG).

Have people walked alongside you recently to encourage you through a difficult time? If so, call them today and thank them for their willingness to let God use them to help you.

Have you used what God taught you in your pain to help somebody else? If not, you still can.

That's what Bill Wilson did. He found his own freedom helping others. And he knew the key to successful sobriety was people helping people, so he set up sponsors to walk with fellow alcoholics through their pain, failures, and discouragement.

But he didn't find the solution until he found the Freedom Giver during his fourth trip to the hospital.

One key to unlocking the mysteries of God's Word is to cry from the depths of our pain, *Why? Why, O Lord, have You forsaken me? Why are You doing this to me?*

Those who are saved will spend eternity in heaven because of pain: Jesus' pain. He had to endure it to save the world, crying out, "My God, my God, why have you forsaken me?" (Mark 15:34).

You cannot become like Christ without pain. Rest assured that God can and often does use your pain and disappointments in surprising ways.

Sydna Masse is an extraordinary woman. As a 19-year-old college student, she discovered she was pregnant. An unsupportive boyfriend led her to choose abortion. She's not alone. About half of American women have experienced unintended pregnancies, and at current rates, more than one-third (35 percent) will have abortions by age 45.[10] Among women having abortions in the United States, about one-half have already had a prior abortion.[11]

Though abortion seemed like an easy solution to Sydna's unwanted pregnancy, it wasn't. Instead, it led to years of grief that began with the birth of her second child. As she held her child in her arms, she grieved the child she never got to hold. Her pain ultimately led her to begin Ramah International, a postabortion ministry. Today, she serves as its president, giving of herself to help other women heal. It took courage for her to admit the sorrow of her past, but God is capable of redeeming any situation.

Your best friend may have had an abortion, or your neighbor, a coworker, or the woman you sit next to in choir. Or maybe you are in that number. If you still carry pain because of that decision, regardless of how long ago it was, let me speak directly to you.

God is the Freedom Giver and wants *you* to experience freedom. He sent Jesus so that we could have life "to the full" (John 10:10). The burden you may continue to feel serves as a warning signal. Any shame that bubbles up at the mention of abortion can bind you, as can the emotional scars you may carry or any sadness that creeps into your heart occasionally. That's not what God wants for your life. You can begin healing right now. All you have to do is ask. When you do, I encourage you to pour out your heart to Him. Though He already knows the circumstances surrounding your decision, acknowledge what you were feeling at the time, how you feel now, how the decision affected you in the past, and how it continues to affect you today. Then, ask Him specifically to release you from the burden you're carrying. Trust that He will be faithful to respond to your request.

Ponder these words: "Before I was afflicted I went astray, but now I keep Your word" (Psalm 119:67 NASB).

A woman's life has many potential areas of pain. We've looked at alcoholism and abortion. But those are just two issues that cause pain and disappointment. We haven't addressed abuse, anorexia, bulimia, depression, infertility, other addictions, promiscuity, or marital infidelity, to name just a few.

Though pain is plentiful in this life, God's willingness to redeem pain is infinite. Will you let Him redeem yours? Your healing may well lead to some of the most meaningful relationships you'll ever enjoy, "for even the Son of Man did not come to be served, but to serve, and to give his life as a ransom for many" (Mark 10:45).

Live the
DREAM

God can and often does use our pain and disappointments in surprising ways.

JOURNAL
PROMPTS

- ❧ Do you need to let God redeem any pain in your past? If so, are you able to acknowledge that pain and begin the process with God?
- ❧ Would you lessen your own pain if you talked about it with someone else? If so, who could you talk with?
- ❧ How can you use your own pain to help others in a similar situation?

Day 5

The Power of Influence

You are who you spend time with.
Tim Clinton

The day Tim and I left Megan at kindergarten was really hard for us. Her hair was up in a bow, and her lunch box was at her side. We sat her down at her desk, got out her crayons, made small talk with the teacher, and kissed Megan goodbye.

Then it sunk in—this was her first day with someone we really didn't know. Someone who would teach her and influence her from this day forward for as many waking hours as we had with her, if not more.

The people you spend time with shape you and influence the way you think, feel, act, and react.

Who or what is shaping you? Tim and I have worked hard to help our children choose their friends wisely because we know peers are such an influence on young people. Lately, I've pondered the importance of choosing friends wisely as adults too. Though peers may not influence us as much as they do our children, they do hold weight in our lives. We must be sure that it's not deadweight that creates an unnecessary burden or a negative influence.

Philippians 4:8 tells us, "Finally, brothers, whatever is true, whatever is noble, whatever is right, whatever is pure, whatever is lovely, whatever is admirable—if anything is excellent or praiseworthy—think about such things."

Do the meaningful relationships in your life allow you to think about these things? Or do they cause you worry, despair, and anxiety?

Make a mental list of those closest to you and ask yourself if each individual has a positive, negative, or neutral influence on you. When you identify someone whose influence is negative, you may be tempted to end the relationship with her. But doing so may cause you to miss the opportunity to speak into her life and be a positive influence on her, even if she is a negative influence on you. The key is identifying these individuals and making sure you are careful and balanced when you're around them so your influence on them is greater than their influence on you.

Let me tell you about a young woman named Allison (not her real name). The summer between her junior and senior year of college, she met a guy in a local coffee shop. He was six years older than she. She was flattered when he bought her a latte, and after an hour of stimulating conversation, she shared her phone number with him. He called the next day. She was thrilled.

The two fell into a relationship that would last throughout the summer and most of her senior year, even though she returned to college, which was in a different city. Steve was thoughtful, kind, and considerate. He wrote long love letters and called daily. He sent special "thinking of you" gifts. He was easy to talk to, had a great sense of humor, and had a wide variety of interests. He was one of the few suitors she had who actually attended church with her. There was only one problem.

Allison wanted to be a virgin on her wedding night, but Steve kept pressuring her to have sex. She began to dread seeing him because she knew the battle would be the same. After some heavy kissing, she would once again have to fight him off and answer the question he asked every time she resisted his advances: "Don't you love me?" Allison tried to explain that she did. She asked Steve to weigh her actions as proof: She responded to his calls, wrote letters in response to his, and caught a ride to her hometown whenever possible to see him.

It wasn't enough, however. Steve gave her an ultimatum: Sleep with him "or else."

Allison chose the "or else," and the relationship ended. Her influence on Steve did not, however. A month after their breakup, she learned from her brother that Steve continued to attend church with her family in her absence. Two months later, he invited Christ into his heart, became a Christian, and was baptized.

Though it was too late for his relationship with Allison, it wasn't too late for Steve. He had been influenced by her faith, which eventually led him to discovering his own belief in God.

I'm interested in this story for two reasons. First, Allison realized that though Steve had a lot to offer in their relationship, ultimately his presence in her life was negatively influencing her. For her own well-being, she ended the relationship. You and I may be called to make a similar decision at some point in our lives—maybe more than once. Proverbs 27:12 says, "The prudent see danger and take refuge, but the simple keep going and suffer for it." We must be prudent when we see danger in our relationships.

Ending unhealthy relationships is hard. But undoing the damage they may do to us is often harder. Consequently, to enjoy meaningful relationships, we must be wise when choosing whom to spend time with.

The second reason I shared this story is that though Steve wasn't a good influence on Allison, she was a good influence on him. Had she not spent time with him, she wouldn't have led him to the Christian faith. Our relationships are like that too. We don't know who will come to faith or when, where, or why. We can't force faith on someone else, so we must simply be willing to share our own faith story and to answer any resulting questions. God will take care of the rest.

After identifying the negative influences in our lives, we must also go a step further and ask ourselves if the good influence we can be in these instances is worth remaining in the relationship.

We all will face times when our relationships get crazy, times when we know that they will adversely affect our own lives. Here are some basic principles that will help you analyze your current relationships:

Be honest with yourself. We can easily turn a blind eye to situations and circumstances in this life. Get an outside perspective if you need to.

Determine the level of others' influence. Are you angry a lot more? Critical? Negative? Are you soft with things you used to be firm on? Has your behavior changed? Are you treating others differently?

Evaluate the relationship in light of Galatians 5:22. Does it reflect the fruit of the Spirit (love, joy, peace, patience, kindness, goodness, faithfulness, gentleness, and self-control)?

You become like the people you spend time with. As you evaluate your earthly relationships, remember that we all need to soak up a little more of Him as well.

Live the
DREAM

*Meaningful relationships require being wise
when you choose whom to spend time with.*

JOURNAL
PROMPTS

- ❧ Who is a negative influence in your life right now? (Be honest!)
- ❧ Are you negatively influencing anyone? If so, what can you do to change your influence?
- ❧ How can you rely on God more fully in your relationships?

Week 4

Secrets to Handling Testosterone

God created man before woman, but then again, you always make a rough draft before creating the final masterpiece.

Menstruation. Menopause. Mental illness. Have you noticed most of the problems we have in life start with "men"?

I heard this joke a few years ago and couldn't help but laugh. The universal sentiment of women toward men seems to be, "Can't live with 'em; can't live without 'em!" Think about it. The men we love the most seem to make us crazy! But then again, where would we be without our fathers, husbands, brothers, and sons to influence, serve, love, and protect us?

Men may be a real problem for you. You may be angry, disappointed, or even disengaged from men entirely. Statistics tell us that about one in every three women reading this book will be physically or sexually abused by a husband or boyfriend at some point in her life.[1] That doesn't include the children who have been victims of neglect or physical, sexual, or emotional abuse by their fathers.

We're all created in God's image, both male and female (Genesis 1:27). He designed us both for a reason—relationship. In fact, the only thing "not good" in the first two chapters of the Bible was that man was alone. Without woman, God's plan for man was not complete. He needed a helper, somebody to support him, so God suggested a "helper suitable for him"

(Genesis 2:18). The Hebrew word for "helper suitable" may surprise you—it literally means "opposite." It means you were created to come alongside and complement the man in your life. Not to be the same as him, not to be inferior or superior to him, not even to be equal to him, but to complement him. It's God's plan.

This chapter is about God's design for relationship with the men in your life. We'll identify the differences between men and women that often get in the way of fulfilling relationships, talk about sex, and focus on relational stumbling blocks and how to overcome them.

Day 1

Making Your Differences Work for You

*Nevertheless, each individual among you also is to love
his own wife even as himself, and the wife must see to it
that she respects her husband.*
EPHESIANS 5:33 NASB

In Men Are Like Waffles—Women Are Like Spaghetti, Bill and Pam
Farrel describe the minds of men and women.

Men Are Like Waffles

We do not mean that men "waffle" on all decisions and are
generally unstable. What we mean is that men process life
in boxes. If you look down at a waffle, you see a collection
of boxes separated by walls. The boxes are all separate from
each other and make convenient holding places. That is typically how a man processes life. [Men's] thinking is divided
up into boxes that have room for one issue and one issue only.
The first issue of life goes in the first box, the second goes in
the second box, and so on. The typical man lives in one box
at a time and one box only. When a man is at work, he is at
work. When he is in the garage tinkering around, he is in
the garage tinkering. When he is watching TV, he is simply

watching TV. That is why he looks as though he is in a trance and can ignore everything else going on around him. Social scientists call this "compartmentalizing"—that is, putting life and responsibilities into different compartments...

Women Are Like Spaghetti

In contrast to men's waffle-like approach, women process life more like a plate of pasta. If you look at a plate of spaghetti, you notice that there are lots of individual noodles that all touch one another. If you attempted to follow one noodle around the plate, you would intersect a lot of other noodles, and you might even switch to another noodle seamlessly. That is how women face life. Every thought and issue is connected to every other thought and issue in some way. Life is much more of a process for women than it is for men.

This is why women are typically better at multitasking than men. She can talk on the phone, prepare a meal, make a shopping list, work on the agenda for tomorrow's business meeting, give instructions to her children as they are going out to play, and close the door with her foot without skipping a beat. Because all her thoughts, emotions, and convictions are connected, she is able to process more information and keep track of more activities.[2]

Spaghetti and waffles. It's a wild example of describing a very important truth—men and women are just plain different. It's like the old "Me Tarzan, you Jane" thing we learned as kids. Despite their differences, Tarzan and Jane found a way to swing gracefully through the trees together. The sooner we can learn how to make this magic happen for us, the more peaceful things will be around our homes.

For Chase and Callie, the first six months of marriage were unusually smooth and problem free. Then, demands from his boss to meet an important fiscal deadline had Chase working late into the evenings, leaving Callie home alone. She began feeling less and less important as Chase's job began consuming him. But Chase knew the deadline would soon pass and things would be back to normal. When he was at home, he tried hard to connect with Callie. But she had already grown frustrated and felt as though he wasn't trying hard enough to meet her needs. They often fell asleep nitpicking or in a deadening silence.

On the day of the deadline, he left work early and brought home a box of chocolates, new lingerie, and a bouquet of flowers. For him, this would be the end of the fighting. As he walked through the door with gifts in hand, she met him with a nasty glare. The message she received was that all he wanted was sex. She, on the other hand, felt alone. Feeling rejected and as if he could do nothing to please her, he retreated to the garage to work on his car.

Most of us can relate to this story of two people who genuinely love one another and want to connect but can't. Callie wanted more time together with her husband and felt misunderstood by the gifts. He felt rejected.

Why can't we seem to get it right with the men we love?

I believe it's because we're literally opposites. Women were created to support the men in their lives and men to protect the women in theirs. We were created to complement and sustain one another. Because we were created for different purposes, we have different needs.

Dr. Willard F. Harley Jr., in his book *His Needs, Her Needs,* outlines some of these most important differences:

- She can't do without affection.
- He can't do without sexual fulfillment.
- She needs him to talk to her and hold conversation.
- He needs her to be his playmate and do things with him. (Harley refers to this as recreational companionship.)
- She needs to trust him totally. Honesty and openness are critical to the relationship.
- He needs an attractive wife. (That means you should take pride in your appearance and look good for him.)
- She needs financial stability and support.
- He needs peace and quiet at home.
- She needs him to be a good father and remain committed to the family.
- He needs her to be proud of him.[3]

Think about this list for a moment. Look at the number of diametrically opposed needs between men and women. He needs peace and quiet at home; she needs conversation. No wonder you get ticked off at your husband when he doesn't want to talk. He's not giving you what you need. And he in turn gets aggravated because you won't leave him alone.

He needs sexual fulfillment to connect emotionally. You need affection in order to desire sex. But if you don't feel close to him to begin with, he ain't gettin' any.

But look at the list again. His way of building intimacy and feeling close is to play with you. To take you fishing, hiking, or to a sporting event. When you decline his invitation to play, the feeling he has is similar to yours when he refuses your invitation to a romantic dinner and sappy love movie.

He needs you to respect him. Paul told the church at Ephesus, "Husbands, love your wives...the wife must respect her husband" (Ephesians 5:25,33). According to Emerson Eggerichs in his book *Love and Respect*, nowhere does the Bible tell wives to love their husbands; it says to *respect* them. He needs to know you are proud of him. The degree to which you feel loved is the degree to which he feels respected. Respect your man, and he is sure to give you the love you need.

Shaunti Feldhahn, author of *For Women Only*, shared with me that "We women usually *do* respect the men in our lives and have no idea that all day long we are doing things that send them the opposite message. We don't realize that when we do something as simple as saying, 'Honey, please stop and ask for directions,' or 'Don't try to fix that. Let's just call a plumber,' what he hears is 'I don't trust you,' or 'I don't believe in you.'"[4] In other words, we don't always realize that our words and actions are making our men feel unloved because they make them feel disrespected.

In your attempts to love and respect him, keep in mind that he is different from you. "Accept one another, then, just as Christ accepted you, in order to bring praise to God" (Romans 15:7). It isn't always easy, but ultimately, it's the key to being successful—in marriage and in life.

You can't fix a problem you don't see. Sharing your needs openly and honestly with one another will open your eyes to the differences between the two of you. When you understand them, you are able to experience and appreciate them at a whole new level. When you do, your attempts to love him are no longer aimless. And as he understands you better, his pursuits will make you feel loved.

Live the
DREAM

Understanding and responding to the needs of your man brings about the intimacy and connection you long for.

JOURNAL
PROMPTS

- ❧ What's the biggest lesson you've learned about relating to the man in your life?
- ❧ Based on what you learned in this lesson, what steps must you take next to transform your most important relationship?
- ❧ How have you misinterpreted your husband's actions and needs in the past?

Day 2

Change Your Man

He has made everything beautiful in its time.
ECCLESIASTES 3:11

Tim and I had a rough start to our marriage. We didn't communicate well. Come to think of it, we didn't do much of anything well. And of course it was all his fault.

So I set about trying to change him. And to my disappointed surprise, nothing I did worked!

Honestly, we were pretty hateful at times in the way we spoke to each other. Much of it was due to our youth and immaturity. Some of it was due to our circumstances. We were both going to school full-time and working. We didn't spend much time together, and the time we did spend was focused on our differences, heightening the conflict. And we weren't communicating what we needed from each other.

At one point, we actually separated. Tim was in the Army Reserves and left town to fulfill a training commitment. We put our things in storage, and I went home to Montana. When I look back, I realize that could have been the end of our marriage. I'm so grateful it wasn't.

After training, Tim called my dad and said he'd do whatever it took to make our marriage work. I know that must have been difficult for him to do. He drove 36 hours nonstop from Virginia to Montana to get me. Driving through South Dakota, he was so tired he literally drove with his head hanging out the window. When he arrived, we decided together that divorce was not an option for us and never would be.

I too made an important decision. Despite my controlling, perfectionistic tendencies, I decided that changing Tim wasn't my job. It was his job and God's job. My job was to work on changing myself. The truth is, the only person you can change is you. Jesus spoke boldly about this:

> Don't pick on people, jump on their failures, criticize their faults—unless, of course, you want the same treatment. That critical spirit has a way of boomeranging. It's easy to see a smudge on your neighbor's face and be oblivious to the ugly sneer on your own. Do you have the nerve to say, "Let me wash your face for you," when your own face is distorted by contempt? It's this whole traveling road-show mentality all over again, playing a holier-than-thou part instead of just living your part. Wipe that ugly sneer off your own face, and you might be fit to offer a washcloth to your neighbor (Matthew 7:1-5 MSG).

A physical law says, "For every action there is an equal and opposite reaction." The same is true for human behavior. The way you approach people triggers certain kinds of reactions from them.

Satisfying relationships between people require a willingness to do two things: First, you must be willing to clearly and graciously explain to other people what they are doing that bothers you. Then, if they choose not to change their behavior, you must be willing either to remove yourself from the situation or to change your response to the behavior. It's that simple— and that complicated. In order to change a man, you must change yourself. When you change, he'll change too.

When I stopped nagging Tim, he began to relax more around me. When I stopped getting in his face, he began to listen more carefully. When I stopped complaining and started complimenting instead, Tim began to blossom as a husband—but I needed to change my own behavior first.

I know you may get tired of always giving and not getting. I'm not talking about tolerating meanness, but about looking inward and asking yourself if you have developed negative patterns of your own. Have you fallen into a mundane, complacent lifestyle? Are things not getting done that used to? Do you need to be encouraged?

I want to end with the most important thing you can do to change your man: Pray for him. "And this is the confidence that we have toward him, that if we ask anything according to his will he hears us. And if we know that he hears us in whatever we ask, we know that we have the requests that we have asked of him" (1 John 5:14-15 ESV).

The only person who can change your man is the Holy Spirit. And we already know "He makes intercession for the saints according to the will of God" (Romans 8:27 NKJV).

So rather than beat him up because of his idiosyncrasies, pray for him. Then take encouraging steps in your own life that enhance your personality, physical health, and emotional and spiritual well-being. When you do, you may be surprised at how your personal change leads him to change.

Learning this lesson helped save my marriage.

Live the
DREAM

You cannot change your man. You can only change yourself.

JOURNAL
PROMPTS

- ❦ Are you hoping to change a man in your life? If so, how can you move your focus from changing him to changing yourself?

- ❦ What areas of your life do you need to begin changing that would help your man grow?

- ❦ Are you guilty of nagging, yelling, and complaining? If so, what could you replace these ineffective techniques with?

Day 3

Stand By Your Man

Behold, I am the LORD, *the God of all flesh;*
is anything too difficult for Me?
JEREMIAH 32:27 NASB

Roxanne Gardner never anticipated that her husband, a former state wrestling champion, would one day be paralyzed from the chest down.

Tamara Carlson (not her real name) had no way of knowing that her fiancé, Tad, would be severely wounded and disfigured by a car bomber in Iraq before he became her husband.

Sheila Amberlain (also not her real name) had no idea that the "additional workload" her husband was supposedly carrying was actually his cover for a midlife marital affair.

Pain and adversity can easily strip us of energy and heart. All three of these women have been challenged by difficult circumstances, and all three made courageous decisions to stand by their men. They know two important things about their relationships and adversity—who they are and where they're going. First, with their husband, "they are no longer two, but one" (Matthew 19:6). And secondly, "in time of need" they know to "boldly" approach the "throne of grace" to "obtain mercy" (Hebrews 4:16 NKJV). Blindsided by the storms of life, they now offer hope and encouragement to women with relational challenges.

For Greg and Roxanne Gardner, the morning of January 11 started as just another day. But it didn't end the way it started. On that unusually foggy morning, Greg left for his morning jog. While running, he was hit by a vehicle and taken by ambulance to the hospital with a broken leg. But his condition steadily worsened, and by the end of the day, he was paralyzed from the chest down.

While struggling to absorb the news herself, Roxanne had the tough job of telling the couple's three girls that their father might never walk again. Then she set about the difficult task of learning what she needed to know to care for her husband. She oversaw the renovation of their two-story house to accommodate his wheelchair and learned how to watch for additional dangerous complications from his injury.

Roxanne recalls her first unsuccessful attempt to help Greg transfer from his wheelchair to the bed. Sure that she could handle it even though he outweighs her, Greg talked her in to helping him make the transfer. Roxanne was mortified when she lost her grip on him and Greg slid to the floor between the chair and the bed, unable to move. Then she panicked. *How am I supposed to get him up?* she recalls thinking. Undaunted, Greg reminded her about the workmen who were renovating their home and calmly asked her to get them to assist him. It was the first of many experiences that required Roxanne to begin a new way of thinking. Now her mantra is, "I can, and I will."

Tamara Carlson's mantra is the same. Her husband, Tad, is one of the 20,000 troops wounded in Iraq. When a car bomber disabled his truck, Tad was engulfed in flames and blinded in one eye. His skull was shattered, riddling his brain with shrapnel. Doctors later removed his right arm below the elbow and three fingers of his left hand. Tad was also disfigured beyond recognition—his ears, lips, and most of his nose burned away.

When Tamara learned of her then-fiancé's injuries, she flew from her home to an Army medical center with one suitcase and a week's worth of clothes. She lived there well over a year.

She's learned how to handle dressing changes, feeding, and personal hygiene." Though Tad is independent, she still buttons his pants because that's one thing he's not able to do.

Now settled into the home Tad bought before departing for Iraq, the couple is navigating the white waters that the first year of marriage brings. Tad took a medical retirement, and Tamara is furthering her education.

Together, they are looking ahead to the future, hoping that the worst is behind them.

Sheila Amberlain didn't think twice when her husband began logging extra hours at work. His job had always required a varying seasonal workload. Only when a friend shared how she learned of her own husband's affair did Sheila begin to have suspicions. She told her husband about the conversation with her friend and was devastated when he confessed to an affair of his own.

Until now, her marriage had been a strong one—or so she thought. Sheila and her husband were extremely compatible and enjoyed each other's company. They spent time together with their children and a wide circle of friends, enjoyed similar pursuits, and had recently helped each other through the death of one of each of their parents. Yet the bond was not strong enough to hold when a coworker began aggressively pursuing her husband. Though he was wracked with guilt, he responded to her flirtations and the excitement offered by a new romance. One thing led to another, and soon he was arranging clandestine meetings planned around his children's sporting events.

When she learned the truth, Sheila wanted to throw him out of the house. But she knew her response would help determine the future of her marriage—or lack thereof. In despair, she locked herself in the bathroom and dropped to her knees on the cold tile floor. Between sobs, she cried out to God and asked for His wisdom and guidance. Almost immediately, an uncanny peace settled over her. Though her initial reaction was that her marriage was over, she realized she had a choice. She could let current circumstances undo a relationship that had 26 years of history behind it, or she could work to salvage it.

Though Sheila was deeply hurt and her self-esteem was shaken, when her husband asked for forgiveness and a second chance, she gave it to him. He ended the affair and immediately began looking for another job to remove himself from further temptation. He held himself accountable to Sheila by letting her see his cell phone and text message bills each month to assure her that the affair had indeed ended. He also began coming home immediately from work each evening, bringing work home with him when necessary but never staying late at the office. His willingness to accept responsibility for his actions and to work to regain Sheila's trust empowered her to forgive him. Recently, when talking to a friend, she said, "We both realize what we almost lost, and things are better than they've ever been between us."

Difficult, life-changing circumstances. Extraordinary courage. These three women realized that though life was testing them in ways they never could have anticipated, they could choose their responses, and their responses would determine the course of their lives.

Whether you're in difficult circumstances or not, the power of choice and courage is a combination that all extraordinary women wield wisely. Problems are not the real issues in life; rather, what we choose to do with them will determine the future. When the storms rage, press in close to Jesus—He will safely guide your steps home.

Live the
DREAM

Extraordinarily difficult circumstances require extraordinary courage.

JOURNAL
PROMPTS

- ⚜ What circumstances have you had to deal with in your relationships that you didn't expect?
- ⚜ What tough decisions have you had to make in order to preserve and further these relationships?
- ⚜ How do the stories of the women in today's reading encourage you?

Day 4

Your Sex-Starved Man

*Anybody who believes that the way to a man's heart is
through his stomach flunked geography.*
ROBERT BYRNE

Sex is to men what oxygen is to women. That may not come as a surprise
to you, but what might be a surprise is *why* sex is like oxygen. We assume
that men benefit physically from an act that women tend to benefit from
more emotionally, but recent research reveals that sex fulfills powerful emotional needs for men as well.

Shaunti Feldhahn interviewed more than 1000 men prior to writing
her book *For Women Only*. Though she wasn't surprised that the interviews
revealed that men desire more sex, she was surprised by the reason why.

> Men want more sex than they are getting. And what's more,
> they believe that the women who love them *don't seem to
> realize that this is a crisis*—not only for the man, but for the
> relationship...For your husband, sex is more than just a phys-
> ical need. Lack of sex is as emotionally serious to him, as, say,
> his sudden silence would be to you, were he simply to stop
> communicating with you. It is just as wounding to him, just
> as much a legitimate grievance—and just as dangerous to
> your marriage.[5]

Sex is as powerful emotionally for men as it is for women but for different reasons. Women want to feel close to a man *before* sex, but men feel close to women *during* sex. Pay attention to this difference. Many couples have trouble connecting sexually because of it. When you don't understand one another sexually, you run the very high risk of not connecting emotionally. And what could add some spice to your relationship becomes a battlefield and a power match where he's always keeping score—"We've only had sex once in the past three weeks."

But understand that in his eyes, sex is like oxygen to the relationship. He can't breathe without it.

You may think he doesn't deserve it. You may say to yourself, *He doesn't meet my needs, so why should I meet his? I can't do everything around this house and meet his needs too. I don't have enough time or energy.*

This is where I believe we all need to take a deep breath together. The apostle Paul is pretty bold in 1 Corinthians 7:2-5 (MSG):

> Sexual drives are strong, but marriage is strong enough to contain them and provide for a balanced and fulfilling sexual life in a world of sexual disorder. The marriage bed must be a place of mutuality—the husband seeking to satisfy his wife, the wife seeking to satisfy her husband. Marriage is not a place to "stand up for your rights." Marriage is a decision to serve the other, whether in bed or out. Abstaining from sex is permissible for a period of time if you both agree to it, and if it's for the purposes of prayer and fasting—but only for such times. Then come back together again. Satan has an ingenious way of tempting us when we least expect it. I'm not, understand, commanding these periods of abstinence—only providing my best counsel if you should choose them.

Does sex *really* mean that much to men? Psychologist Kevin Leman thinks so. I chuckled when I read this, and you might too.

- A sexually fulfilled husband will do anything for you.

- A sexually fulfilled husband is a scriptural mandate.

- A sexually fulfilled husband will feel good about himself.

❦ A sexually fulfilled husband will take on his life work with unmatched vigor and purpose.

❦ A sexually fulfilled husband appreciates the important things in life.[6]

Let's be honest here, Kevin. When a man is sexually satisfied, he is probably more able to satisfy his wife's needs, but that doesn't mean he always will. (One thing's for sure—at least he'll sleep better!)

But I've got to be honest—this is a mutually beneficial arrangement. When Daddy's happy, or if Daddy thinks he's going to get happy, things tend to get done a whole lot more quickly around the house. Many women make the mistake of waiting until things are "good" in their marriage before they initiate sex. But when we refuse to have sex, we're preventing the emotional closeness we receive as a result. This enormous paradox has chilling repercussions when it is not understood. Suffocate the sexual part of marriage, and you suffocate the relationship. Nobody can breathe.

I love what Gary and Barbara Rosberg write in their book *The Five Sex Needs of Men and Women:*

> The reality is that we often want the same things. Our deepest desire, whether we're male or female, is ultimately to become one. He wants intercourse; she wants intercourse. He may want physical intercourse more than she does, and she may want emotional intercourse more than he does, but when a couple can meld physical and emotional intercourse, they will find the pathway to great sex.[7]

To add some spice, I've included some true aphrodisiacs:

Tenderness. Good sex starts by caressing your lover's heart. It was never meant to be a single act of expression or feeling. Sexual satisfaction begins with gentleness, understanding, acts of kindness, and self-sacrifice. Treat one another well, and you'll discover a new kind of sexual satisfaction.

Time. Good sex is about taking time—not just during sex—to show your lover you care for and love him. African writer Ernestine Banyolak beautifully illustrates this:

> A man's experience is like a fire of dry leaves. It is easily kindled, flaring up suddenly and dying down just as quickly.

A woman's experience, on the other hand, is like a fire of glowing charcoal. Her husband has to tend to these coals with loving patience. Once the blaze is burning brightly, it will keep on glowing and radiating warmth for a long time.[8]

Touch. Good sex requires that you touch him often. Give back rubs, hold hands, kiss, hug, and caress one another. It's sure to take your intimacy to the next level.

Talk. Good sex speaks clearly and gently about caring for, accepting, and valuing your husband. Be sure to express your heartfelt needs and feelings before, during, and after lovemaking.

The next time you're frustrated because he's not getting anything done around the house, and he's complaining he's going to die without sex, go find your raincoat and high heels. You'll be shocked at what he gets done in the next 30 minutes!

Live the
DREAM

Gentleness, understanding, acts of kindness, and self-sacrifice all combine to become the building blocks of sexual satisfaction.

JOURNAL
PROMPTS

- Read and study Proverbs 5:15-19; Song of Solomon 7:10-13; 1 Corinthians 7:3-5; and Hebrews 13:4.

- Are you guilty of seeing sex as a duty or withholding it to punish your husband? If so, how can you shift your thinking?

- Make a list of things you can do today to begin adding spice to your sexual life with your husband.

Day 5

I Hope You'll Dance

Dancing is a wonderful training for girls. It's the first way you
learn to guess what a man is going to do before he does it.
CHRISTOPHER MORLEY

I pushed him away and slammed the door, making it very clear to Tim
that the flowers he just brought me were not what I wanted. With a despon-
dent yet agitated look on his face, he turned around and threw the flowers
on the floor. They were Tim's gesture at a peace offering for a fight we'd just
had. Instead of accepting it, I overreacted, causing him to do the same. We
had a wonderful time "in the Spirit" together, if you know what I mean.

The early years of marriage teach us a lot. In a way, it's like learning to
dance. If you watch the show *Dancing with the Stars,* you see finesse and
rhythm as the dancers delicately glide together with the music. But the
beauty in the dance doesn't happen overnight. It takes practice. Hours
upon hours of practice.

Early on, the man will step on his partner's foot. She in turn may head
left when he is leading her right. Only after dancing together awhile and
learning one another's idiosyncrasies will they begin to accurately anticipate
what's next on the dance floor. Marriage is similar—it takes two parties
moving in the same direction and anticipating each other's moves to be
successful.

But stumbling blocks litter the way—things we do that take the stride out of the dance. And when we can't get it right, we become frustrated and irritable. If our partner blames us for the breakdown, we get defensive and blame back. Dissension creeps in, and the relationship is divided.

Recognizing obstacles is important to the health and vitality of your relationship. Some obstacles include expecting your husband or boyfriend to be a mind reader, not clearly stating your needs, holding on to unrealistic expectations, and putting children ahead of your marriage.

Men are not mind readers. But often, we expect them to be. I expected Tim to know that flowers wouldn't be enough to patch up the fight we'd had. I wasn't being fair by expecting him to know that. And I'm not being fair when I expect him to know when I think he's not carrying his own weight with family matters, or when I need a break from my household responsibilities, or when I disagree with a decision he's made if I haven't articulated my concerns.

Over the years, I've heard many women say, "I shouldn't have to ask," or "If I have to ask, it doesn't count." Maybe it's clear to you that someone needs to take out the trash or empty the dishwasher. But your man is a waffle who compartmentalizes each aspect of his life, so he may not notice these things as easily as you do. You're naturally able to think about more than one thing at a time. Getting angry isn't nearly as effective as developing a method of communicating that works for both of you.

Your man cannot meet your needs if he doesn't know what they are. This seems simple on paper, but in reality, many of us expect our spouses or significant others to be mind readers, and because of that, we don't take the time to verbalize what we need or want, leading to the second threat of not clearly stating your needs. Expecting him to meet your needs but keeping them a secret isn't fair. The whole idea seems ludicrous when you see it on paper, doesn't it? Yet expecting men just "to know" is exactly what many of us do every day. Then we're surprised and angry when our husband or boyfriend misses the nonverbal clues we've been dropping.

Instead of keeping things to yourself, get in the habit of using the "I feel…when…because…" formula for communicating your needs.

"Honey, I feel *frustrated* when *you read the paper immediately after dinner while I clean up* because *it feels unfair to me*. I'm usually responsible for meal preparation, so could you help me clean up so we could sit and read the paper together?"

By starting with an "I statement," you lessen the chance that your spouse will immediately feel defensive. By stating what you feel and why you feel it, you help him understand your emotions. When you clearly articulate your needs, the people you love are more likely to meet them.

Your spouse could possibly refuse to help and continue reading the paper after dinner, but at least he knows how he's making you feel. If he's unwilling to help, other, more serious issues could be putting your relationship in jeopardy.

In the example above, the wife isn't asking much of the spouse, and the expectation to help clean up after dinner is not unrealistic. However, if he grew up in a home where food preparation and cleanup was "woman's work," this might be a big deal to him. If so, perhaps the couple could negotiate another solution to the situation. Instead of reading after dinner, perhaps he could agree to take the dog for a walk or to spend time helping the children with homework so that her burden for the evening is relieved in some way. Then, before bed, the couple could read the paper together.

This is a simplistic example, but it demonstrates the problem: Expecting sudden, big changes in your spouse simply isn't fair. If he hasn't been helpful or romantic the first 15 years of marriage, he's not likely to start now. Change is possible, but you need to ask yourself if what you're expecting is realistic. If not, lowering or changing your expectations makes more sense than walking around mad all the time because he isn't meeting them.

Unmet expectations are a cause of much distress in marriage. But another stumbling block can also cause distress. Sometimes you don't even know you're guilty of doing it, but when you do, it has the potential of building a wall that blocks the intimacy between you and your husband. The stumbling block is this: consistently placing your children ahead of your marriage. Doing so can destroy the very foundation of a healthy family.

Please don't confuse what I'm saying here. I'm not saying you shouldn't be invested in your children; on the contrary. Rather, I'm saying you shouldn't exhaust all your resources of time and energy on them and sacrifice your relationship with your husband. God calls us first to be wives. Then he gives us children. This is by design so that children have the security of being parented within the context of a healthy partnership, not at the expense of it. A healthy marital relationship fosters a safe environment for children. And when a child's world is safe, he or she is easier to parent. This places less strain on your family and adds more blessing.

Overcoming these obstacles is not always easy. Living by 1 Peter 3:8

(NKJV) is a great way to start: "Finally, all of you be of one mind, having compassion for one another; love as brothers, be tenderhearted, be courteous…"

Be of one mind. Even though you and your husband will not agree on everything, you should work toward having one mind. Compromise is essential in living this out.

Have compassion. When you know you truly care for one another, you're able to share your deepest thoughts and feelings with each other.

Love. This seems obvious, but love can be the most difficult thing to maintain. Know the love described in 1 Corinthians 13.

Be tenderhearted and courteous. Have an attitude that puts your husband's needs ahead of your own—even when you're exhausted.

Practice these principles, and I bet you'll be dancing with your husband in ways you never dreamed possible.

Live the
DREAM

A selfless attitude is the foundation for overcoming obstacles in your relationships with men.

JOURNAL
PROMPTS

- What needs do you have that you have not yet articulated to your husband?
- How have you expected your husband to be a mind reader lately, and what was the result?
- Do you agree that families should be marriage centered? If so, how can you focus more on your marriage in the coming days, weeks, and months?

Secrets to Mastering Your Emotions

Let's not forget that the little emotions are the great captains of our lives and we obey them without realizing it.
Vincent Van Gogh

Elizabeth, exhausted from a rough week with her kids, snapped at her boss when he asked her about a project she had been late on.

When Kelly saw her 17-year-old daughter, Tegan, walk into the room, she just knew something bad happened at school that day.

Johanna, at wit's end with her husband, Jim, locked herself in the bathroom and refused to talk any further.

Have you ever said something rash and wished you could take it back? Do you have a knack for knowing when somebody is hurting? Can you relate to the woman who locked herself in the bathroom because of a fight with the man she loves? Maybe you've cried over a stupid movie or laughed uncontrollably over something that wasn't really funny.

If you're in a relationship at all, you will feel things. God made us that way. Anger, sadness, grief, discouragement, fear, love, jealousy, and happiness are all emotions we know well—sometimes for good and sometimes for bad. When life seems unfair or we have too many demands, too much tension, and too many unpredictable circumstances, we can feel crazy.

When stressed, I want to run, sleep, clean, shop, or (most of all) eat choco-late—lots of it!

One of our strengths as women is our ability to respond to our emo-tions and to notice others' feelings as well. But this can also be one of our weaknesses. Anger can rule us, depression may overwhelm us, fear might paralyze us, and insecurity will keep us from being all that God created us to be—if we let them.

Much of what burdens and binds women today occurs on the inside, where thoughts are born and take flight. These thoughts have the ability to lift us higher, rid us of unwanted habits, and encourage us to take the high road when those around us won't. They can also weigh us down, trap us in regrets of the past, and stunt our personal growth.

The challenge in mastering emotions is to seek contentment even in the midst of life's storms and unwanted circumstances. In this chapter we'll examine a variety of emotions and learn how we can master them.

Day 1

Seeing Red

*Anger: an acid that can do more harm to the vessel in which it
is stored than to anything on which it is poured.*
SENECA

I remember the e-mail Tim and I received from a friend of ours shortly
after his wedding. It told of a crystal vase he and his wife had received as
a special wedding present, a vase that was very special to her. The e-mail
also told about their first real fight they had as newlyweds. He wrote that
in the heat of an argument, "I got stupid and so angry that I grabbed that
vase, threw it across the room, and it split into a million pieces. It was awful.
Since then it's gone downhill." In a Charlie Brown–style postscript at the
end of the e-mail he wrote, "Marriage...ugggggghhhhh."

Conflict in relationships is inevitable. Anytime you bring two people
together, often from very different backgrounds, and put them in close
proximity, they will experience conflict. But the issue really isn't fighting.
The way you fight is what matters, the way you work to resolve differences
and challenges between the two of you. In fact, researcher and marital
expert John Gottman wrote that sometimes those who fight well tend to
love well too. On the other hand, show me a home where people are out
of control and all you see is conflict, and I will show you a marriage that's
filled with anger, resentment, bitterness, and pain. Being on the receiving
end of someone's anger is no fun.

Learning how to manage your anger and frustration individually and as a couple will go a long way in helping you build a healthy relationship. I have no doubt that the level of your closeness and intimacy will never rise above the level of your conflict and fighting.

Sometimes conflict is fueled by anger. Be careful—"Speak when you're angry, and you'll be sure to make the best speech you'll ever regret."[1] You may also damage relationships beyond repair, do things you wouldn't normally do, and create unexpected trouble for yourself. That's because what we do in our anger is usually sinful and hurts deeply.

Yet anger also has a positive side. As a God-given emotion, it is best understood as a "state of preparedness" to respond to real or perceived wrongdoings or injustices in our lives. It alerts us when someone is taking advantage of us or treating us unfairly. Anger gives us the courage to stand up for ourselves or our loved ones. And it creates the energy we need when we must work for change—either in our lives or in others'.

Anger is a powerful emotion. We can harness it for good or use it for evil. It can be a catalyst for positive change or a stubborn reason to stay the same. It alerts us to others' shortcomings and our own often unrealistic expectations.

Jesus can relate. He showed His anger in John 2:13-16:

> When it was almost time for the Jewish Passover, Jesus went up to Jerusalem. In the temple courts he found men selling cattle, sheep and doves, and others sitting at tables exchanging money. So he made a whip out of cords, and drove all from the temple area, both sheep and cattle; he scattered the coins of the money changers and overturned their tables. To those who sold doves he said, "Get these out of here! How dare you turn my Father's house into a market!"

Jesus was fired up about the violation going on in His Father's house. But He responded appropriately. We, on the other hand, usually don't and subsequently hurt those around us. Getting control of and managing our anger is not always easy, especially in a stressed-out world where people easily get ticked off and flip out. Many have learned the power of anger to control and manipulate others.

I must be careful when I'm angry because, as the old Chinese proverb says, "If you are patient in one moment of anger, you will escape a hundred days of sorrow." That's why Ephesians 4:26 is so important. It literally says,

"In your anger do not sin." You can be angry. You can respond to the situation, but temper your response, for "a fool gives full vent to his anger, but a wise man keeps himself under control" (Proverbs 29:11).

Michelle McKinney Hammond, author of *The Power of Being a Woman*, observes, "Any time we respond out of anger or fear it is usually the wrong response and the clean up and repair is extensive, if possible at all. Allow yourself to get to a place of calm objectivity before addressing something that causes you concern or warrants a response."[2]

Here's how to keep your anger from damaging your relationships:

Recognize it. What makes you angry? What happens to you physically when you get angry? What do you do with the anger? You can begin managing your anger by noticing its pattern in your life and being honest about it. You can't change what you don't understand. Do you yell? Cry? Get critical? Get even? Go silent? Recognizing what triggers anger in you and how you respond to it is the first step to getting control.

Slow it. Once you recognize that you're angry, find ways to respond appropriately and not react foolishly. You may need to take a personal timeout to separate yourself from the situation. Go exercise to release some tension, talk to a trusted friend, or write your thoughts and frustrations in a private journal. The Word says, "Better a patient man than a warrior, a man who controls his temper than one who takes a city" (Proverbs 16:32). Do what it takes to grow in patience.

Manage it. "Be quick to listen, slow to speak and slow to become angry" (James 1:19). You may have to remove yourself from the situation for a while before you try to resolve the hurt and restore the relationships involved. If yelling is your nature, learn to speak quietly and slowly. Empathize with those who hurt you. Do not seek revenge.

Resolve it. Develop a plan to use the anger for deeper spiritual growth and sanctification. Pray and surrender it to the Holy Spirit (Galatians 5:16) and forgive those who have wronged you. As you do, "Let all bitterness, wrath, anger, clamor and evil speaking be put away from you," and instead "be kind to one another, tenderhearted, forgiving one another, even as God in Christ forgave you" (Ephesians 4:31-32 NKJV).

Live the
DREAM

In your anger, don't sin. Respond, don't overreact.

JOURNAL
PROMPTS

- ✣ Are you currently angry about something? If so, verbalize it in your journal by identifying why you are angry and planning proactive steps to help you deal with your anger constructively.

- ✣ What activities release anger and tension in your life? Do you routinely engage in these activities?

- ✣ Could any anger from your past be affecting you now? Write a prayer to God, telling Him what you're angry about and asking Him to help you work through it.

Day 2

Faces of Fear

Courage is resistance to fear, mastery of fear—
not absence of fear.
Mark Twain

We live in uncertain times and have plenty to be afraid of. Terrorism, economic collapse, unemployment, nuclear armament, identify theft...and that's just the beginning.

Bowling Green State University has identified the "Top Ten Fears That Keep People from Getting What They Want in Life:"

1. fear of failing
2. fear of success
3. fear of being judged
4. fear of emotional pain
5. fear of embarrassment
6. fear of being alone/abandoned
7. fear of rejection
8. fear of expressing our true feelings
9. fear of intimacy
10. fear of the unknown[3]

Do you struggle with any (or all!) of these fears? If you can't find one there, check out this list of the top ten phobias:

1. arachnophobia (the fear of spiders)

2. social phobia (the fear of being evaluated negatively in social situations)

3. aerophobia (the fear of flying)

4. agoraphobia (fear and avoidance of any place or situation where escape might be difficult or help unavailable in the event of developing sudden panic-like symptoms)

5. claustrophobia (the fear of being trapped in small confined spaces)

6. acrophobia (the fear of heights)

7. emetophobia (the fear of vomit or vomiting)

8. carcinophobia (the fear of cancer)

9. brontophobia (the fear of thunderstorms)

10. necrophobia (the fear of death or dead things)[4]

In addition to these, if you speak to a group of women, they would probably add these: outliving one's spouse or not finding a mate; infertility, miscarriage, or child health issues; not being able to protect one's children; having enough money to retire; marital infidelity and/or divorce; caring for aging parents. (I was tempted to add "wrinkles" to the list, but compared to the above, they didn't seem so bad after all!)

With so much to be afraid of in our world, it's hard not to worry. But listen to Jesus. He tells us, "Do not worry about tomorrow, for tomorrow will worry about itself" (Matthew 6:34). This seems easy for Him to say, but what about when tough times come, such as when this month's mortgage payment is due and you have no money? In the midst of the fear, refocusing on Christ and realizing that He really does understand what we're going through is not easy.

When fear begins to creep into our minds and drain our souls, we can easily lose focus on the One who gives courage. To regain focus and truly feel His love, we need to remind ourselves that He is the God of the angel armies and that Jehovah Jirah—which means "the LORD will provide"

(Genesis 22:14)—cares for us. I have always been encouraged by the biblical names for God and their meanings. Here is a partial list. Meditate on each one and ask God to fill your heart with His grace and truth.

> Elohim, "Mighty One" (Genesis 1, Psalm 68)
>
> Adonai, "Sovereign, Ruler" (Psalm 6, Isaiah 68)
>
> Yahweh or Jehovah, "I Am Who I Am" (Exodus 3:14)
>
> El Shaddai, "God Almighty" (Genesis 17, Exodus 6)
>
> El Elyon, "God Most High" (Genesis 14, Psalm 9)
>
> El Olam, "Eternal God" (Genesis 21, Isaiah 40)
>
> Jehovah Jireh, "the LORD Provides" (Genesis 22)
>
> Jehovah Sabbaoth, "Lord of Hosts" (Joshua 5, 1 Samuel 1)
>
> Jehovah Raah, "the Lord Our Shepherd" (Psalm 23)[5]

I'm comforted as I read this list. In the face of fear and uncertainty, I know that the One who cares for me is God Almighty, the Most High, the Mighty One, the Lord of Hosts.

Imagine yourself in the wilderness with one change of clothes, no makeup, and no contact with the outside world—certainly not my typical idea of a women's retreat. But for two extraordinary women, Gina Murrow and Donna Claus, the setting is perfect for helping rid women of fear. Having seen so many women live lives of fear and apprehension, the two decided to begin leading wilderness retreats for the sole purpose of helping women identify and relinquish their personal fear. The retreats are called No Fear Forwards.

What makes modern women want to stay on a glacier, flip kayaks in 34-degree water, stay in tents in the same woods as bears, and learn to shoot guns and use a map and compass? It may be the opportunity to get away from the drudgery of regular life for four days or the chance to challenge themselves. More likely, however, it's the opportunity to fully face their fears and banish them once and for all.

Though physical activity is a big part of each Forward retreat, emotional activity is an essential element as well. During the retreat, each woman is placed on the "hot seat," and the group focuses on her unique questions, dilemmas, and faith. Donna Claus leads this portion of the Forward, which is designed to help women identify why they are not living a full and trusting life in God. Claus relies heavily on the Holy Spirit for this. The results are incredible.

Says Murrow, "I've seen marriages saved, relationships with kids improved, careers changed, and whole attitudes about life drastically reversed...God always surprises us." Claus echoes Murrow's observations: "I have husbands stop me at church and tell me that their marriages are changed. I listen to kids and hear them say they have a different mom. That is what makes me want to go ahead with more. We are seeing lives changed!"

Before leading others to live fearlessly, Gina and Donna both had to overcome a host of their own fears. They did so (and continue to do so) by relying solely on God. Donna notes, "The major problem I see is that life is not about us. When we think that we are the reason for life, we live in fear. When we want everything our way, we live in fear. If women can go away from these Forwards with one idea, it should be that 'life is not about me.' Only when we leave the lie behind can we live fearlessly with our God. God had to wrench that out of me. It was painful; it was horrendous. But once I realized that all that matters is God and His plan, I found the secret to fearlessness. The opposite of fear is faith."

Gina and Donna are teaching women to choose to worship Jehovah Jireh when they lack something in their life, El Shaddai when their fear is too great to handle on their own, and Adonai when they are ready to surrender their own plan in order to focus on God's plan.

Rely on faith in the face of fear. I'm not quite ready to do the wilderness trip, but I do know that fear strips us of power, and we need to increase our faith to win over our fears.

Live the
DREAM

With God, you can face your fears and find His peace.

JOURNAL
PROMPTS

- ⚜ Which of the fears listed in today's reading did you identify with? (You can list more than one if necessary!)

- ⚜ Have you been challenged by fears that weren't listed? If so, please list them.

- ⚜ What specific steps can you take to let faith replace fear in your life?

Day 3

Bad Hair Days, Fat Days, and Feelings of Insignificance

The opposite of security is insecurity,
and the only way to overcome insecurity is to take risks.
THEODORE FORSTMANN

Growing up, most girls struggle with their looks and feelings of self-worth. Remember the horn that popped up on the absolute tip of your nose—the one you were sure everyone in the whole school could see from 50 feet? As adult women, we still often feel less than adequate. Bad hair days. Fat days. Not feeling loved, cared for, appreciated, or worthwhile. We work hard to keep our lives and our families' lives balanced. But the rewards often seem limited—very limited. And when we're not rewarded, we can sometimes feel as if what we're doing is meaningless and that we are worthless. If we are not careful, these feelings can lead to poor decisions, mistakes, and regrets.

We are insecure when we are not confident or feel unsafe. But that safety has nothing to do with the environment we're in or the people around us. Instead, it has everything to do with how we see ourselves. Most of the time, the way we see ourselves is based on our performance or on the way we think others see us. That's a prescription for disaster. Our focus must be on Christ and what He sees in us.

I know of a girl dating a pastor from California. She lives in Alabama.

Both are very creative and are constantly finding ways to stay close despite the distance. She received a Valentine's gift from him a few days early and could hardly wait to open it. When the long-anticipated day finally arrived, she woke early. As she unraveled the bow she found a note slipped inside:

> When you have a bad hair day,
>
> When you wake up on the wrong side of the bed,
>
> When you feel insignificant, lesser than, doubt your worth,
>
> Always remember!

Inside the package was a key chain. Engraved on one side was the word "Wonderfully." The other side simply read, "Fearfully." Because he's not there in person to remind her of her worth and who she is in Christ, he made sure she had a daily reminder.

You too should have a daily reminder.

Why? Because you begin to build your self-worth by understanding how much God really loves you.

But unfortunately, most women don't believe God really does love them. Even if we say we believe it, we don't live as if we do.

What am I talking about? Most of the women I know can cite Bible passages reminding them of their worth in Christ. You probably know those verses too—Jesus' assurance that even "the very hairs of your head are all numbered," that God cares even for small birds, that "not one of them will fall to the ground apart from the will of your Father," and that "you are worth more than many sparrows" (Matthew 10:29-31). Or that you are "fearfully and wonderfully made" (Psalm 139:14).

We say we believe these things, yet we do things that contradict what we say we believe. If we really believe we are fearfully and wonderfully made, why are we constantly comparing ourselves to others?

"Look how thin she is."

"She is so organized."

"I wish I were as close to the Lord as she is."

We do ourselves and those we compare ourselves to a grave injustice. Rarely do we compare ourselves to somebody we see as inferior to us. We measure ourselves against those we see as better than us or those who have something we want.

Comparing leads to coveting, to envying others for what they have.

Wishing you had her money, her looks, her body, her good fortune, her favor. I've done it myself. And this insecurity is like a cancer that consumes the heart. You start to feel sorry for yourself and jealous of the life others live. When this happens, resentment and bitterness can take root. We can even become angry at God for making our life less appealing than others' lives.

The only way to stop the cancer of insecurity from spreading is to find contentment, to live out the truths of who we are in Christ. Here's how:

Look back and be honest. Where do your insecurities come from? Were you bullied growing up? Did you somehow get the message that you just aren't quite good enough? Did you always have to perform to be loved? Did family dysfunctions or secrets cause you to live in fear as a child? Have repeated disappointments led you to believe you just don't have what it takes?

You can begin to release the hold insecurity has on you by being clear about what you are insecure about, accepting responsibility for it as your own, and turning it into a positive motivator for thinking about yourself in an admirable way.

Be thankful, pray, and think. Freedom comes by way of godliness and by living according to Philippians 4:8: "Whatever is true, whatever is noble, whatever is right, whatever is pure, whatever is lovely, whatever is admirable—if anything is excellent or praiseworthy—think about such things."

Thinking on what is pure and lovely, admirable and noble, empowers you to think accurately about who you are. When you're feeling insecure and you start comparing yourself to others, you need to stop, recognize what's going on, clean up your thought life, and move forward.

See the value of others. Comparing yourself to others can be instructive when you use it as a constructive motivator for positive change in your life. It's also instructive when you're willing to examine yourself and ask, "Why do I feel this way?" More importantly, you have to answer the question honestly and then listen to what you learn about yourself through the answer.

The musical *My Fair Lady* is about a common flower girl who becomes the project of a learned professor. He takes her under his wing, educates her to speak properly, and teaches her manners. His confidence in her leads to her own confidence in her newly learned skills. As a result, she blossoms. Little by little, her insecurity and feelings of unworthiness fall away.

As you dig deeper in the Word and see all that God has created you to be, your insecurity will also fall away. Your status as a child of the King will begin to eclipse the specifics of life that led to your insecurities in the first place. You will see yourself and the events in your life in a whole new way when you understand that regardless of how insecure you feel, how bereft or lost you feel, or how painful life gets, God created your innermost being and knit you together in your mother's womb. Meditating on His confidence in you will help build your own self-confidence.

When insecurity threatens, remember that you are fearfully and wonderfully made.

Live the
DREAM

*As God's daughter, you are beautiful in His eyes,
and He loves you with an everlasting love.*

JOURNAL
PROMPTS

- What's currently causing you to feel insecure? Name everything that's challenging you in this regard.
- How can you turn these issues into positive motivators for change?
- Read Psalm 139. Pray over verses 23-24 and ask God to help you see yourself the way He sees you.

Day 4

Freedom from Depression

Is anyone crying for help? GOD is listening, ready to rescue you.
If your heart is broken, you'll find GOD right there; if you're kicked
in the gut, he'll help you catch your breath. Disciples so often get
into trouble; still, GOD is there every time.
PSALM 34:17-19 MSG

Have you or someone you love ever battled depression? You'd be shocked at how many women have or currently are. If you answer yes to five of the nine symptoms below, and the symptoms last two weeks or more, you may want to read this very carefully. The good news is that you can overcome depression.

Have you had any of the following?

1. deep feelings of sadness
2. a marked loss of interest or pleasure in activities you once enjoyed
3. changes in appetite that result in weight losses or gains unrelated to dieting
4. insomnia or oversleeping
5. loss of energy or increased fatigue
6. restlessness or irritability
7. feelings of worthlessness or inappropriate guilt

8. difficulty thinking, concentrating, or making decisions
9. thoughts of death or suicide or attempts at suicide [6]

Depression is all too common. It affects nearly one in ten adults each year and nearly twice as many women as men. An admission of depression once met with judgment and gossip, but it now often results in an affirmative head nod and understanding. Although the stigma surrounding depression is fading, the cases of it are not.

According to the American Psychiatric Association, depression can affect anyone. Several factors can play a role in the onset of depression:

Biochemistry. Abnormalities in two chemicals in the brain, serotonin and norepinephrine, might contribute to symptoms of depression, including anxiety, irritability, and fatigue.

Genetics. Depression can run in families. For example, if one identical twin has depression, the other has a 70 percent chance of experiencing it as well.

Personality. People with low self-esteem who are easily overwhelmed by stress or who are generally pessimistic appear to be vulnerable to depression.

Environmental factors. Continuous exposure to violence, neglect, abuse, or poverty may make people who are already susceptible to depression all the more vulnerable to the illness.

Medical conditions. Illnesses such as a brain tumor or vitamin deficiency can also cause depression.

Postpartum depression. Rapid changes in hormonal levels after pregnancy may prompt symptoms of depression.

Perhaps you wrestle with depression or have a loved one who does. Rather than being concerned about what other people will think if they find out, invest your energy wisely by seeking help and beginning the road to healing.

Some biblical characters seemingly suffered from depression, giving us insight and encouragement when we wrestle with it ourselves or help loved ones walk through what may be a short valley or a lifelong struggle. If you've been touched by it in some way (and most of us have, either through our own lives or the lives of loved ones), see what you can learn from the life experiences of these spiritual giants. Take time to read through these passages to discover how each of them battled depression.

Abraham (Genesis 15)

Jonah (Jonah 4)

Job (Job 38–42)

Elijah (1 Kings 19)

Jeremiah (Jeremiah 1; 9; 13)

David (Psalm 6; 13; 39; 42–43; 51; 55; 62; 69; 88; 116; 130; 142)[7]

David lamented, "I am troubled, I am bowed down greatly; I go mourning all the day long...I am feeble and severely broken; I groan because of the turmoil of my heart" (Psalm 38:6,8 NKJV). These aren't the words of a carefree, happy-go-lucky man. Instead, they reflect a heavy heart, one that may have been suffering from symptoms of depression.

In addition to a heavy heart, those who struggle with depression may worry about their daily work and family commitments, their friends' and families' reaction if they find out, and the best way to address it.

Some people believe those who follow Christ shouldn't, don't, or won't get depressed. But not one of us is immune; we are all susceptible. Those who hold to this misleading notion may in fact add to the burden of those who are depressed.

Dave Dravecky was a pitcher for the San Francisco Giants when he discovered a cancerous tumor in his pitching arm. His arm was amputated to keep the cancer from spreading. The journey from healthy and noted ball player to former ball player without an arm obviously was difficult. And though Dave's wife, Jan, stood steadfastly by his side while he battled cancer, she began a battle of her own with panic attacks, anxiety, and depression.

Like others who have walked this path, she began an unplanned journey. She writes, "I had never known anyone who had experienced something like this, and as a committed Christian, I didn't understand how this could be happening to me. Guilt engulfed me. I felt alone, confused, and scared. I needed a lifeline. I needed to be shown the way up and out."[8]

For some, the way up and out comes through the passage of time. For others, it includes therapy. Medication helps some. Others benefit from a combination of the three. Why depression happens matters less than what to do about it when it does happen.

If it has happened to you, get help. If it has happened to a loved one, join the journey by offering practical, emotional, and spiritual support. In either case, acknowledge that God can and does work though depression. You can gain new insights and deepen relationships. God can work in the midst of depression.

Life is difficult. It looks even more so through the eyes of one who's depressed. The Bible offers hope:

> We are hard-pressed on every side, yet not crushed; we are per-plexed, but not in despair; persecuted, but not forsaken; struck down, but not destroyed (2 Corinthians 4:8-9 NKJV).

> Therefore we do not lose heart. Though outwardly we are wasting away, yet inwardly we are being renewed day by day. For our light and momentary troubles are achieving for us an eternal glory that far outweighs them all. So we fix our eyes not on what is seen, but on what is unseen. For what is seen is tem-porary, but what is unseen is eternal (2 Corinthians 4:16-18).

We may be hard-pressed, but we are not crushed because the God of the universe is on our side.

Live the
DREAM

By fixing your eyes not on what is seen (the temporary things of the world), but on what is unseen (the eternal things of heaven), you can overcome depression.

JOURNAL
PROMPTS

- How has depression touched your life?
- A burden shared is a burden lessened. If you are challenged by depression, who is trustworthy enough to share the burden with you?
- How can you walk alongside someone you know is experi-encing depression?

Day 5

Contentment

Happiness isn't having what you want;
it's wanting what you have.

"Content"—it literally means "desiring no more than what one has; satisfied."[9] Do you know someone who lives with such freedom? Contented, satisfied, settled, and fun to be around? I need more of that in my life.

Paul was an unlikely ambassador for Christ. Before becoming a follower he actively persecuted Christians (Acts 9:1-2).

But it's just like God to turn one of His enemies into an ardent follower. As Saul was on his way to Damascus, a light from heaven flashed, and he heard God ask, "Saul, Saul, why do you persecute me?"

"Who are you?" Saul asked. The answer he heard was clear: "I am Jesus, whom you are persecuting."

Later, Saul would become God's chosen instrument to carry His name before the Gentiles and their kings and before the people of Israel (verse 15).

How wild it must have been for Saul to hear from the very God he was persecuting! But God didn't just issue a cease-and-desist order. He filled Saul with the Holy Spirit, and the Bible tells us, "At once he began to preach in the synagogues that Jesus is the Son of God" (Acts 9:20).

A persecutor becomes a servant. Hatred becomes love. One day he's *after* Christians, and the next day he *is* one. What irony!

The same irony often filters through modern-day life. In Jesus, bro-kenness finds healing. Hopelessness finds hope. Weakness finds strength. As we grow in faith, we learn that God is present in the unexpected, the unimaginable, and the unbelievable. Paul's story doesn't end with his con-version. In fact, it just begins. His ministry came with a high price. He was flogged, beaten with rods, stoned, shipwrecked, and imprisoned (2 Corin-thians 11:24-27). Yet amazingly, he says, "I have learned the secret of being content in any and every situation, whether well fed or hungry, whether living in plenty or in want. I can do everything through him who gives me strength" (Philippians 4:12-13).

Despite his hardships, Paul was content. He was confident in Jesus and recognized that his strength came from the Lord. With this strength, he could face his pain and the mountains in his life with a new peace.

As Henry Blackaby wrote, "God's always given his people assignments that are too big for them to handle alone so that a watching world can see not what *we* can do—but what *God* can do."[10]

Our job is to be content with our life and the assignments we're given and to do them to the best of our ability, trusting God's strength to make it possible. This is not easy. Contentment is not a natural emotion for most of us. It is something we must strive for.

When emotions threaten to overwhelm us, we must realize that God is in every circumstance and everything we feel. He's present in our anger, fear, insecurity, and depression. He's our strength when we feel the job is too big or we can't go on. Rest in Him and find the contentment that only He can give.

Live the
DREAM

The strength you need to do whatever is before
you comes directly from the Lord.

JOURNAL
PROMPTS

~ What current circumstances in your own life call for contentment?

~ In what way does searching for contentment in the midst of tragic or difficult circumstances seem contradictory?

~ What assignment do you feel is too big for you to handle right now, and how can you let God's strength carry you through it?

Week 6

Secrets to Handling Imbalance

*Women need real moments of solitude and self-reflection
to balance out how much of ourselves we give away.*
BARBARA DE ANGELIS

Living a balanced life seems next to impossible. Just when I think I have everything in my life in order, Tim adds something to the schedule, Megan or Zach tell me at the last minute about something I need to attend at school, the computer crashes, somebody gets sick, or the car breaks down. I am sure you can relate. When it rains, it pours.

I chose to write about handling imbalance in our lives—rather than balance—simply because I believe the idea of finding and living a balanced life promotes a dangerous myth that compels many women to feel as if they're doing something wrong or that they just don't have their act together when things don't run smoothly. Learning how to respond to the obstacles in life in a healthy way seems to make more sense than trying to control that which we often can't control.

The good news is that Jesus is with us every unexpected step of the way (Matthew 28:20). He's with us day and night, in our coming and going, and in the natural imbalance that occurs throughout the course of each day. He sees us struggling to keep all of our plates spinning and watches as we wear ourselves out trying to be all things to all people. Then He speaks words of comfort: "Come to me, all you who are weary and burdened, and

I will give you rest" (Matthew 11:28). How comforting is that? I certainly need it.

Whether you are balanced or not, God is on your side, and He has much to teach you about caring for yourself so that you can care for others.

Day 1

Connecting with God

There is a vast difference between saying prayers and praying.

It is morning, and I am in my car, parked in the lot at my children's school, which is about 20 minutes from our home. That's 40 minutes round-trip. On some days I wish they attended the school closer to our home, but I'm committed to the commute because I believe in the value of this particular school and in what our kids are learning there.

Each school day is the same. We start with breakfast, followed by the mad dash to get out the door. I help both Megan and Zach make sure they have what they need for the day as we hustle to the car to begin the trek together. I am thankful every day for that car ride—just me and my kids together with no distractions, enjoying beautiful moments of discussion as we zip through the winding roads of our Virginia countryside.

Sometimes when Tim is out of town we use the car ride as a time to call and connect with him as a family. Sometimes we pray for the five children our family sponsors through World Vision and Compassion International Zach, Megan, and I often take turns praying out loud in the car for those who we know need it.

After dropping off the kids at school, I turn off my cell phone, park the car, and sit in silence in the parking lot. The car is my sanctuary on wheels. I can open the Bible and read or write in my journal. I can bow my head in prayer. Sometimes, I just sit and listen for His quiet whisper in response to the pleadings of my heart. Some days, instead of speaking or listening, I simply read, letting other authors encourage me with what they've learned and are learning about God.

I know that this is the quietest my day will be. Once I put the car in gear and pull into traffic, my life becomes a rush of activities and responsibilities. I'm consumed with the desire to cross off all the items on my to-do list even though I add more items as I think of them throughout the day. Pick up the dry cleaning. Go to the grocery store. Let the dog out. Start a load of laundry. Let the dog in. Take care of duties for upcoming Extraordinary Women conferences. Return phone calls. Take Zach to get new baseball cleats. If I'm not careful, I'll become consumed by the busyness of life—so much so that I might forget to take a look around in order to see who's on the journey with me and to notice their needs.

As I turn the key in the ignition and the engine springs to life, I often think about the lives of pioneer women in this country. Instead of walking to the garage and hopping in a car, women went to the barn to hitch the horses for a ride into town. Instead of enjoying a smooth ride as I do, the women who came before me bounced along on a wooden wagon bench. Instead of relaxing in a temperature-controlled interior, they squinted through the dust that the horses kicked up. So much has changed since those earlier days. The luxuries we have now make life immeasurably easier. You'd think that making time for a God connection each day would be easier, and yet as things have gotten easier, we've gotten busier. That's why my quiet moments are so important and why I sit in my rolling sanctuary to hear His voice before the day begins.

Some days are easy, but most days require a lot. When we talk to God *before* the day gets started, we're better able to handle whatever happens during the day. The connection doesn't have to be formal or lengthy. Even fleeting thoughts turned heavenward can keep our connection with God intact.

God loves us and listens to us. He's never too busy or unavailable. Yet often we're too busy and unavailable for Him. That's when our imbalanced lives threaten to overwhelm us. The imbalance often leads to more busyness and less time for Him. When this happens, we can spiral downward. The busier we are, the harder we work to catch up. The harder we work to catch up, the faster we move. The faster we move, the less time we have for prayer. The less time for prayer, the more likely we'll try to handle things on our own. The more we try to handle things on our own, the heavier the burden. The heavier the burden, the more we need Him.

We can wait for the downward spiral of busyness to knock us down before we decide it's time to get back to God, but a much more sensible decision would be to let Him carry us through the imbalance so we don't get pulled into the resulting whirlwind to begin with. That way, we don't have to spiral downward before finding Him again. We simply rest in His arms as we tackle what's before us.

In her book *Having a Mary Heart in a Martha World,* Joanna Weaver writes, "'I can't spend time with God today,' I may rationalize. 'I haven't the time.' But the truth of the matter is this: The rougher the day, the more time I need to spend with my Savior. The more hoops I have to handle, the more I need to keep my center."[1]

God blesses the moments I take from my schedule each day and multiplies them before giving them back to me. My return on this investment is divine, and somehow I always have enough time. Starting each day by connecting with God has another benefit as well: Once I start a conversation with Him, I don't want it to stop. As I pull into traffic after my quiet time, my mind is buzzing with thoughts, ideas, and questions. I know that the conversation I begin with Him in the morning will continue, and because of that, I know I'll have what I need to get through the day.

Live the
DREAM

*Even fleeting thoughts turned heavenward can
keep our connection with God intact.*

JOURNAL
PROMPTS

⚜ What kind of "God connections" are you making each day, and how are they helping you get through the imbalance of life?

* Has the "busyness spiral" happened in your life (or is it happening now)? If so, how can you keep from being pulled into the whirlwind?

* Joanna Weaver writes, "The rougher the day, the more time I need to spend with my Savior." Are you in the habit of turning to God first on your toughest days?

Day 2

Invest Your Time Wisely

Whatever you do, work at it with all your heart.
COLOSSIANS 3:23

I love what consultant Peter Drucker has to say about setting priorities: "There is certainly nothing so useless as doing with great efficiency that which should not be done at all."

Do you ever feel guilty at the end of the day for wasting time? You beat yourself up because you needed to get some things done, and you just didn't do them. And the things you did do didn't matter anyway. Add to tomorrow's list the things you didn't do today, and now you feel even more overwhelmed—and paralyzed.

As your list grows, you don't even know where to start. So you don't. You put off things you should do because you don't have enough time, and the things you are doing ultimately have no value. When we don't prioritize our to-do list, we waste more time in the long run. When we believe everything on our list is important, or when we haven't taken the time to identify what's essential, we become most susceptible to becoming overloaded.

Investing time wisely is a matter of constant personal reflection—being mindful to determine the things we should do and being willing to let go of the things we shouldn't do. It's a matter of letting your yes be yes and your no be no (James 5:12). The difficulty for most of us is recognizing when to say yes and when not to. You can do this only when you know what you value and why. Identifying your values will determine your course of action.

Before King Xerxes named Esther his queen, she was orphaned as a child and raised by her uncle, Mordecai. When Mordecai became aware of a plot to destroy the Jewish people, he asked Esther to approach the king to ask for help.

When I think of a queen, I think of a woman married to a king and empowered with all the rights that position holds. In Esther's case, however, she was able to go to the king only when he summoned her because anyone who approached the king without being summoned risked being put to death. Consequently, Mordecai was asking Esther to risk her life to save her people. Esther responded by requesting that Mordecai and other Jews fast and pray for her for three days. When this time was up, Esther approached the king.

Esther's actions reflected her values. Her priorities were set. When she approached the king, "Esther had kept secret her family background and nationality just as Mordecai had told her to do, *for she continued to follow Mordecai's instructions as she had done when he was bringing her up*" (Esther 2:20). Esther's priority was obeying her uncle and saving her people even if that meant risking her life. As a result, Mordecai was honored and the Jews were saved.

Aware of her values and not afraid to stand by them, Esther knew what she had to do. The same is true in our lives. The people or things that grip the most sensitive areas of our hearts compel us to respond. What do you give yourself to and pour yourself out for? Your children? Your husband? The women you are mentoring? Your mom, dad, sister, or brother? Maybe it's your ministry or job. Knowing what's most important in your life will help you know what you need to do and when.

Emergencies happen, and sometimes family and friends need you more than you need to complete your to-do list. So you drop what you're doing to go to the hospital when a friend has been injured; you make a special trip to the grocery store to pick up ingredients to make dinner for a friend who just gave birth; and you rearrange your schedule to sit with a friend's ill mother so your friend can get her hair done.

Once you know what's important in your life, knowing how to invest your time is easier. God deposits 86,400 seconds into the time account of your life every day. You must use every last one of them, and He hopes you invest them wisely.

How are you using your time? What are you pouring your heart into? Take a personal inventory. Find out where you're investing your time and if the expenditure reflects your priorities.

Most of us are so harried and desperate just to get through another day that we don't take the time to step back and ask ourselves if what we're doing really matters and if our activities reflect our priorities. Often the two are disconnected, though we may be too busy to see it.

Jody Antrim writes, "The two best indicators of whether you're living your value system are your calendar and your checkbook."[2] How long has it been since you've done a self-audit to see if you're living your priorities? If it's been a while, now's the time to grab your checkbook and your calendar and make a midcourse correction.

Remember, you have 86,400 seconds today. Invest them wisely.

Live the
DREAM

*Knowing your values helps you determine
your course of action.*

JOURNAL
PROMPTS

- ❧ How can Esther's story of courage and obedience help shape your personal story?
- ❧ Should you be saying no to anything right now?
- ❧ What priorities do your calendar and your checkbook reflect?

Day 3

What Really Matters

*We are so obsessed with doing that we have no time and no
imagination left for being. As a result, men are valued
not for what they are but for what they do or
what they have—for their usefulness.*

Thomas Merton

The quote above saddens me. Our society seems to have become a sort of manufacturing company. If you are doing your part and keeping up with the assembly line, people like you, and you fit in. If you decide to work a lot of overtime and not use your vacation or sick days, your boss may even promote you and praise you for all you do. But if you can't keep up or simply choose not to, you're expendable. Fitting in seems to be all about usefulness.

Many of us have fallen into this performance trap, believing the more we do, the more we matter. Our self-worth is determined by how many things we get done each day. When we don't get things accomplished, we feel like failures. And we all know failures are expendable.

But God sees you and me differently. As Joanna Weaver writes, "The kingdom of God, you see, is a paradox. While the world applauds achievement, God desires companionship. The world clamors, 'Do more! Be all that you can be!' But our Father whispers, 'Be still and know that I am God.'"[3]

During a visit with Mary and Martha, Jesus noticed that Mary chose to sit and be with Him while Martha busily bustled about in the kitchen, missing time with the One who came to visit. Consumed with preparations and frustrated that her sister sat while she worked, Martha finally snapped and asked Jesus, "Lord, don't you care that my sister has left me to do the work by myself? Tell her to help me!" Jesus replied, "Martha, Martha…you are worried and upset about many things, but only one thing is needed. Mary has chosen what is better, and it will not be taken away from her" (Luke 10:38-42).

Martha prioritized the things she had to get done; Mary prioritized her relationship with Jesus, who taught us a lesson that still applies today: Don't let busyness interfere with relationships. Choose people over things.

I know this is not always easy. I struggle through this imbalance daily because I know that if I only focus on people, my work will never get done. But if I focus solely on tasks, I do so at the expense of relationships. So what's a woman to do?

When life gets overwhelmingly out of balance, we need to be still and know that He is God. In the stillness, ask yourself this question: *What's the best use of my time today?*

Sometimes the best use of my time is running errands, doing laundry, or dusting. Sometimes it's making calls, writing letters, or visiting with friends or family. Sometimes it's closing my office door and focusing on business. The answer differs, depending on the day or week or current circumstances.

But relationships matter everywhere—at work, home, school, daycare, the grocery store, and anywhere else you go. Ask yourself the question frequently and in every context: *What is the best use of my time today?*

In his book *The Seven Habits of Highly Effective People,* Stephen Covey writes, "Next to physical survival, the greatest need of a human being is psychological survival—to be understood, to be affirmed, to be validated, to be appreciated."[4]

When we recognize that life is more than just our to-do list and we start paying careful attention to the needs of those in our life—to be understood, affirmed, validated, and appreciated—we invite balance into our lives. When relationships are troubled, we become imbalanced, overwhelmed, ineffective, and preoccupied. Ironically, when we place people before things, relationships are healthier, and we're more effective in what we do. Though the two seem mutually exclusive, they are closely inter-twined.

Fitting in didn't matter as much to the saints referred to in Hebrews 11 as it does to us. "They admitted that they were aliens and strangers on earth" (Hebrews 11:13) because they saw something beyond the limits of their earthly vision.

Growing up as a Christian I've heard the "being vs. doing" sermon preached time and time again. But when I read an excerpt from Don Piper's book *90 Minutes in Heaven,* I caught a glimpse of what those saints actually saw. That foretaste has given me a new understanding of how to handle the imbalance of being and doing, and it has changed the way I think every day. I now have a clearer understanding of what really matters.

The book is a biographical account of the car accident that took Don's life—for 90 minutes—and his incredible journey from earth to heaven and back. The details of his experience in heaven solemnly reminded me that I really don't belong here in this world. This is not my home.

As Don entered heaven, a crowd of people he knew and recognized welcomed him.

> I gazed at all the faces again as I realized that they all had con-tributed to my becoming a Christian or had encouraged me in my growth as a believer. Each one had affected me positively. Each had spiritually impacted me in some way and helped make me a better disciple. I knew—again one of those things I knew without being aware of how I absorbed that informa-tion—that because of their influence I was able to be present with them in heaven.[5]

This chilled me. I had to do a gut check. How often do we get so caught up with the task at hand that we miss the opportunity to disciple or min-ister to somebody who literally knocks on our door and needs our help? If Don's account is even the slightest bit true, heavenly influence could be knocking at our door without us even realizing it. Are people a priority in your life?

Let me rephrase that in a way that makes you think even more about that question: Are you willing to drop *anything* you're doing at *any moment* for the chance to minister to the heart of the person standing next to you?

Live the
DREAM

*What really matter are the hearts we touch and
the lives we influence.*

JOURNAL
PROMPTS

- Who are the people in your life that you have trouble putting before your to-do list?
- What's the best use of your time today?
- Who needs to be understood, affirmed, validated, or appreciated in your life, and how can you accomplish this?

Day 4

Lightening the Load

It is impossible to get exhausted in work for God. We get exhausted because we try to do God's work in our own way.
Oswald Chambers

I can't tell you the number of times I've done something by myself because I bought into the idea that "if you want it done right, do it yourself." Or the number of times I was too proud to ask for help because I thought I would seem less capable. And sometimes I refused to let others help because doing so would mean losing total control.

When we try to do too many things or refuse help from others, our lives become more imbalanced. And for most Americans, exhaustion has become an epidemic.

- ⚜ Workplace stress costs more than $300 billion each year in health care, missed work, and stress reduction.[6]

- ⚜ Americans work more than 1800 hours on the job a year— 350 hours more than Germans and slightly more than Japanese.[7]

- ⚜ More than 30 percent of workers say they are "always" or "often" under stress at work. A quarter of those surveyed in 2002 said they often did not have enough coworkers to get the job done.[8]

֍ The average European worker gets four to six weeks of vacation per year compared to the average two weeks of vacation for their American counterparts.[9]

We are certainly an overloaded society. Stress piles up, affecting our physical, emotional, and mental health and distorting our attitudes at work, at home, and even in our ministries. Pushed to the limit, we become exhausted and ultimately ineffective in God's work.

Moses knew exhaustion all too well. Attempting to fix the inefficient judicial system set up in the wilderness, Moses tried to shoulder the burden alone. But his father-in-law, Jethro, recognized Moses' inability to handle all of his people's cases, saying, "What's going on here? Why are you doing all this, and all by yourself, letting everybody line up before you from morning to night?"

After Moses tried to excuse himself, Jethro continued, "This is no way to go about it. You'll burn out, and the people right along with you. This is way too much for you—you can't do this alone. Now listen to me. Let me tell you how to do this so that God will be in this with you."

Whoa! Was Jethro really implying that if Moses didn't begin to delegate, God wouldn't be in it? The answer is yes.

From a wise third-party perspective, Jethro saw the danger signs of a leader on the edge of burnout. So he warned Moses that people rise and fall on leadership. If Moses became exhausted, those working with him would falter too. Jethro knew exhaustion comes not from the Lord but from man's stubborn inclination to do things his own way.

Jethro continued, "Be there for the people before God, but let the matters of concern be presented to God. Your job is to teach them the rules and instructions, to show them how to live, what to do. And then you need to keep a sharp eye out for competent men—men who fear God, men of integrity, men who are incorruptible—and appoint them as leaders" (Exodus 18:14-21 MSG).

Jethro advised Moses to delegate his responsibilities. You will need to do the same with the tasks God places before you. He puts mentors, helpers, and burden-bearers in our lives to support us in the work He calls us to do. Before you burn out, look around for the helpers God may have sent your way.

Asking for help is not a sign of weakness. God designed us to be in community with one another, to help when we can, and to accept help when we need it.

So what can you do to lighten your load?

Know your limits. Never let your schedule get so out of control that you can no longer manage it. Do a personal inventory. Are you getting enough sleep? Spending enough time with your children? Your significant other? Learn to recognize the physical, emotional, and mental warning signals your body emits at the brink of exhaustion.

Know God's will. God's will is for you to "pursue what is good both for yourselves and for all" (1 Thessalonians 5:15 NKJV). It's not to scramble around frantically to make sure every task is completed by the end of the day, wearing out both you and those around you. If you're constantly living with an agitated heart, you are not in the center of God's will.

Know when to quit. Jesus never spent His time and energy the way we do today. The Bible gives no indication that He worked around the clock. In fact, in many cases Jesus snuck off alone to pray and rest. Being in God's will, Jesus was able to go to sleep without having healed and saved everybody in Israel.

Know what's important. Knowing your priorities will help you accomplish more even when you feel as if you're doing less. Effectiveness is not about quantity and getting a lot done; it's about the quality of what you are doing and understanding that the Holy Spirit is ultimately responsible for multiplying your efforts.

I don't know what you're wrestling with in your life that might be too heavy for you to bear. But I do know that right now, somewhere in your life, some people are just waiting for you to ask them to help you. Maybe a friend can give you a break from care-giving responsibilities. Or a supervisor will assure that your work gets done as you go through chemotherapy and radiation. Or a credit counselor is waiting for you to call so she can help you begin the journey back to financial health and freedom.

Only you know what's weighing you down. But Jesus stands ready to help you figure out how to lighten the load, and He has placed people in your life to assist you. All you have to do is ask.

Live the
DREAM

Asking for help is not a sign of weakness.

JOURNAL
PROMPTS

- What are you wrestling with in your life that feels too heavy to bear?
- Who can you ask to help lighten your load? (Consider asking your spouse, immediate family members, and friends. Also consider who you might be able to hire to help.)
- Are you more comfortable when you feel you're in control of things? If so, why? Would you be willing to give up control of just one thing this week in order to practice lightening your load?

Day 5

Seasonal Living

Who of you by worrying can add a single hour to his life?
MATTHEW 6:27

Do you believe you must do everything now rather than accept that some things are yours to do now and some are meant to do later?

Do you believe you must do everything you're asked to do or want to do rather than acknowledging that others are capable of helping?

Do you worry about missed opportunities and fear that you won't be asked to participate a second time or at a later date?

If so, consider exploring how your beliefs affect the number of things on your to-do list.

We can engage in two types of thinking: scarcity and abundance. Scarcity thinking is based on the idea that there isn't enough to go around (enough work, enough love, enough money), and abundance thinking trusts that there's plenty. Because scarcity thinkers fear missed opportunities, they have a tendency to say yes to too many things in order to store up for the future. Abundance thinkers choose to believe that whatever they don't grasp right now will be waiting for them at another time. They recognize that the opportunity might look different in the future, but they are willing to accept that.

Most of us are combined scarcity-abundance thinkers: Sometimes we believe there is enough to go around, and sometimes we fear there isn't. Often, the things that matter most to us are the items that fall into the scarcity camp, such as the job we've been working toward for years or the man we've been searching for just as long. The fear that we'll miss out creates an urgency that clouds our thinking and leads us to make poor choices, such as accepting new job responsibilities in the midst of caring for an ill family member or buying a house because "it's such a great price" even though it's beyond our financial means.

Do you believe there is plenty? Or do you operate under the assumption that you need to grab what you can for yourself in case there's not enough to go around, or that you must grab it now while the opportunity is there? Though these are simple questions, understanding your answer can be complicated.

Ecclesiastes 3:1 assures us that "there is a time for everything, and a season for every activity under heaven." Life is a continuum of seasons, and though you may be rearing young children now and thinking you'll never have another adult conversation or get out of the house without spit-up on your shoulder, those times will indeed come. Though you may currently feel trapped by the responsibility of caring for your husband's ill mother, this too is a season. Some seasons are obviously longer, but in time, most pass.

Rather than feeling you need to do and experience everything now, learn to accept that you can grasp some opportunities now and save some for later. This thinking keeps us from piling so many items on our to-do lists and accepting so many responsibilities that we are severely imbalanced.

When we are way out of balance, we often created the unevenness in our lives to begin with. Of course, blaming others for doing so is much easier than accepting responsibility. We say things like "I have to," or "I have no choice," when in fact we do have a choice. We just decide not to exercise it. The cycle continues as long as we let it. Only when we decide the future is going to be different can real change happen.

Jesus addressed scarcity thinking head-on by asking, "Who of you by worrying can add a single hour to his life?" (Matthew 6:27). Worrying that there won't be enough or that the opportunity won't be offered again doesn't add anything to life; it takes away from it. Jesus assures us that the Father cares for us. When we rest in that thought, starting to think abundantly is much easier.

Abundance thinking helps us keep life in balance. Instead of thinking, *If not now, when?* you think, *If not now, later.* Instead of thinking, *If I pass on this opportunity, it may never come again,* you think, *If the opportunity doesn't come again, it wasn't meant to be.*

Abundance thinking also leads you to believe that God will provide whatever you need to get through whatever you must. This knowledge is one of the greatest weapons you have to add balance to your life.

Live the
DREAM

Rather than feeling you need to do and experience everything now, accept that you can grasp some opportunities now and save some for later.

JOURNAL
PROMPTS

⚜ Are you a scarcity thinker or an abundance thinker? How does scarcity thinking contribute to the imbalance in your life?

⚜ How can Ecclesiastes 3:1 help you achieve balance?

⚜ How does knowing that God will provide for you influence your thinking?

Week 7

Secrets to Getting Through Tough Times

Suffering is the true cement of love.
PAUL SABATIER

Life is brutal.

Cancer. Car accidents. Abuse. Domestic violence. Miscarriages. Pain-filled marriages. Divorce. Single parenting. Poverty. Caring for aging parents. An empty nest. Homicide. Suicide. Terrorism. Hurricanes. Tornados and more.

If we are truly honest with ourselves, we have at some point questioned God about such heart-wrenching circumstances. *God, why are You allowing this to happen to me? What did I do to deserve this?* Many of us can relate to David's cry in Psalm 6:6: "I am worn out from groaning; all night long I flood my bed with weeping and drench my couch with tears."

We cannot escape pain. No one has a vaccination for it, and no one is immune. Even the earth itself is in anguish and "subjected to frustration" (Romans 8:20).

Yet in all our pain, Paul says we can "rejoice in our sufferings" (Romans 5:3). But what was he thinking? When our soul is in anguish and we're crying out for the cancer to be removed, the relational brokenness to be healed, or our lonely hearts to be filled with the love we cannot seem to find, joy seems impossible. When I'm hurting I can't even find the energy to do much of anything, let alone find joy.

Yet the pain has a purpose. The earth was subjected to suffering in hope that it would be liberated from bondage (Romans 8:21). Tough times serve the same purpose in our lives. When we are in the midst of painful circumstances, we can hardly see the hope and the light at the end of the tunnel. But God promises us that if we stay obedient to Him, the product of suffering is perseverance and character. These attributes produce joy and a hope that does not disappoint (Romans 5:5).

No journey is as lonely as walking through "the valley of the shadow of death" (Psalm 23:4). But Jesus is the most compassionate Comforter. Difficult times test our faith and require us to rely on others when we are not strong enough to continue walking alone. Though these lessons may be unwanted, they deepen our faith, mature our character, and make the joyful times in our lives even more precious.

Day 1

Why?

Suffering produces perseverance;
and perseverance, character; and character, hope.
ROMANS 5:3-4

Sunday, November 5, 2006, is a night our family will never forget.

The weekend was packed with activity. We had traveled two hours for the final baseball tournament of the year. Our son, Zach, and his best friend, Josh Barrick, played on the team, and their dads were the coaches.

We arrived home from the tournament just in time to get ready for our church's six o'clock service, where our daughter, Megan, and Josh's older sister, Jennifer, were singing in a choir. The choir's presentation was spectacular and the congregation's response enthusiastic. Jennifer's grandfather was the guest speaker. It was an extraordinary night.

After the service, the Barrick family invited family and friends to their house to watch football and celebrate a memorable weekend together. As people arrived at the Barrick home, they sat in the driveway and waited. And waited. The Barrick family never arrived.

Tim had a six o'clock flight the next morning, so we decided to skip the fellowship and go immediately home. A few minutes after we walked through the door, the phone rang. A drunk driver had hit the Barricks' car head-on, and the initial report on their condition was extremely bleak.

When tough times engulf us, well-meaning people encourage us to rest in Jesus and trust that He will take care of it all. But that's easier said than done. In dark times and deep pain we need more than eloquent words. You know as well as I do that when tragedy strikes, it can shatter our expectations of the world and our beliefs about a loving God. When our worldview is shaken to its core, our internal response can range from feelings of complete numbness to a jumble of uncontrolled anger, deep sadness, and bone-chilling fear. And in the midst of the confusing emotions, we naturally ask, *Why?*

Why did this happen to such good people—an entire family who not only loves Jesus but lives purposely to make His name known?

Why were all four now lying in different hospitals, fighting for their lives?

Miraculously, all four family members survived. Josh had the fewest injuries and was back to school about a week later. His parents, Andy and Linda, remained in different hospitals for weeks after being in and out of surgery to repair a plethora of broken bones, damaged nerves, and other serious injuries. Their road to recovery continues.

Jennifer, on the other hand, was the most critical. With a traumatic head injury, she lay in a coma for more than a month. Three months after the accident, she finally returned home. But a different journey had now begun for the Barrick family—a journey they never expected when they left church that Sunday evening in November. Even though she is home, Jennifer still struggles with limited short-term memory and poor eyesight.

Why did this happen to such a beautiful girl with an incredibly bright future ahead of her? Why did God allow this trial to touch this most beloved family?

At some point in your life, you have asked why. We all have.

Job did too. In fact, he was so desperate that he denounced his birth, asking God, "Why did I not perish when I came from the womb?" (Job 3:11 NKJV). Buried in pain, he saw no hope. And he didn't have the strength to look for it, either. When God allowed Satan to take everything Job ever loved and owned away from him, Job cried out, "Where then is my hope? As for my hope, who can see it?" (Job 17:15 NKJV). Looking for anything to help him through, he prayed, "What strength do I have, that I should hope?" (Job 6:11 NKJV).

When we have no energy to find the hope we need and we're not sure how we'll make it through, we tend to ruminate on the *why* question and allow it to torment us. How do we get beyond it?

Pray. When what's before you seems too much to handle, you can turn to God as Job did and ask for the wherewithal to do what's necessary. He's the only thing Andy and Linda have to hang onto. When you simply don't know what to do, you can ask the Holy Spirit to grant you wisdom and insight (James 1:5).

People. You must also surround yourself with a community of people who can help you through the tough times. We were not meant to walk through them alone, and often the biggest mistake we make in difficult life circumstances is refusing help or alienating ourselves from others.

Process. Though you may know in your heart that you can turn to Jesus at any time, many of us are trained to spring into action when something needs to be done. Consequently, we try to work our way out of tough times instead of leaning into them and learning what we can in the midst of the pain. It's all about the process—suffering is about becoming more like Him.

You may never receive the answers to the *why* questions you have. God neither explained Job's suffering nor helped him make sense of his loss. But He did highlight the reality of His sovereignty and His unconditional love for us.

Our love for Him in return cannot be based on how we think He is treating us. He expects us to trust Him and His goodness regardless of what happens to us in life. In the end, Job found peace, not in answers or in different circumstances, but in a deeper desire to live in the presence of God.

The *why* questions become means to an end. And even though the end may not bring the answers you're looking for, once you reach it, you're no longer as concerned about the *why* because something more beautiful and fulfilling has happened—you've experienced life in the presence of God.

May that be the desire of your heart.

Live the
DREAM

Let your why *questions lead to something more beautiful
and fulfilling—a desire to live in the presence of God.*

JOURNAL
PROMPTS

~ List some of the tough times you've been through. What did you learn about God's nature because of these difficulties?

~ The Bible tells us that "suffering produces hope, and hope does not disappoint us." What does this mean to you, and how can you apply it to your life?

~ How have you tried to work your way out of tough times, and what has been the result?

Day 2

The Forgotten Path

Faith is not simply a patience that passively suffers until the storm is past. Rather, it is a spirit that bears things—with resignations, yes, but above all, with blazing, serene hope.

CORAZÓN AQUINO

Have you ever been to one of those prayer meetings where everyone is gathered in a circle, heads are bowed, people may even be holding hands, and the person praying audibly voices a prayer of—you guessed it— patience? James 1 stuff. "Count it all joy when you fall into various trials, knowing that the testing of your faith produces patience." You know what I'm referring to. Particularly if they prayed for you.

The word "patience" has become more than just an ugly word in prayer circles. We've moved now to feeling as if the attribute of patience is a literal curse on our lives. And it's easy to see why. Patience is difficult. In fact, the root word for patience is *patior,* meaning "to suffer."

But we've done ourselves a grave injustice by denigrating this necessary attribute. I sadly admit I agree with what A.W. Tozer said about modern-day Christians (including me):

> I am afraid we modern Christians are long on talk and short on conduct. We use the language of power but our deeds are the deeds of weakness. We settle for words in religion because deeds are too costly. It is easier to pray, "Lord, help me to

carry my cross daily" than to pick up the cross and carry it; but since the mere request for help to do something we do not actually intend to do has a certain degree of religious comfort, we are content with repetition of words.[1]

We all want to get to the next level in our relationship with Christ. That's not the problem. The problem lies in our fear. We're afraid to pay the price to walk the narrow road. I think we too often forget that "narrow is the gate and *difficult is the way* which leads to life, and there are few who find it" (Matthew 7:14 NKJV). I don't know about you, but I want to be one of the few.

I once overheard one of Zach's baseball coaches tell the boys that the best and brightest baseball players are taking 400 to 600 swings of the bat a day. As a mom, I think that's quite crazy to ask of my son. But I also understand that if he wants to get to the next level, he's got to work hard to get there. Statistics reveal that of all boys ages 9 to 14 who play travel baseball, 10 in 5000 get full scholarships to play in college, and only 1 in 5000 makes it to play professionally. The road to the next level is never easy.

Take Christ's journey to Calvary for instance. We may use religious comfort and repetition of words to ease our pain, but Jesus took the narrow, difficult way. He rode into Jerusalem on a donkey (Luke 19:28-40). As Henri Nouwen explains, "Jesus entered into Jerusalem...on a donkey, like a clown at a parade. This was His way of reminding us that we fool ourselves when we insist on easy victories...The way from Palm Sunday to Easter is the patient way, the suffering way."[2]

Jesus did not come to heal all of Israel or take away every pain we experience.

Many of us have forgotten the path we must take to get to the next level in our relationship with Christ. It has been rejected by a society thriving on instant gratification, faster technology, and a fear of commitment. We want it now, or we don't want it at all. Even committing to a two-year cell phone agreement is considered a courageous feat these days. No wonder we balk when we hear the word "patience." Our culture has denied it, and most of us have forgotten it.

To discover God's dream for our lives though, we've got to rediscover the forgotten path. Surely the path is paved with patience, but if you live your life constantly trying other routes, hoping that a quick devotion in the morning and a ten-second prayer for your neighbor with cancer will get you to the next level, you're likely to grow frustrated and resentful. We learn patience as we embrace tough times. As Nouwen posits, "To learn patience is not to rebel against every hardship. For if we insist on continuing to cover our pains with 'Hosannas,' we run the risk of losing our patience. We are likely to become bitter and cynical or violent and aggressive when the shallowness of the easy way wears through."[3]

Learning patience, as Nouwen admits, is not about denying tough times. As we've seen, it's about finding joy "when you fall into various trials, knowing that the testing of your faith produces patience" (James 1:2-3 NKJV). No one wants to have her faith tested in difficult ways, but that's the only way. So when you're angry at God, when you don't understand Him, and when you feel abandoned by Him, know that His reaction does not depend on your feelings or your circumstances because "Jesus Christ is the same yesterday and today and forever" (Hebrews 13:8). He loves you and cares for you and wants you to experience His glorious presence (John 17:24).

Speaker Lois Evans uses an illustration about a silversmith to teach us the value of patience. Silver takes a long time to be refined enough to be workable, and a silversmith can't just put it in the fire and walk away. He knows that he might be working with silver of varying quality, and he has to set the temperature accordingly. Once it's set, he has to stay until he sees his image in the silver.

Notes Lois, "Jesus Christ is going to stay with you in your fiery situation because He's a good silversmith. He's going to stay there until He sees His image and what He's wanting to do in your life become a reality."[4] Jesus is willing to be patient with us, and we must be willing to be patient with ourselves and with our faith as we take the time necessary to move it to the next level.

As those tough times in life come and go, remember the forgotten path…

> even though you have to put up with every kind of aggravation in the meantime. Pure gold put in the fire comes out of it proved pure; genuine faith put through this suffering comes out proved genuine. When Jesus wraps this all up, it's your faith, not your gold, that God will have on display as evidence of His victory" (1 Peter 1:6-7 MSG).

When you're facing difficult times, remember the hope found in the Easter story. Life can come after loss, and we can bear it because of Christ. The question isn't whether you will have tragedy and loss in your life. Those are givens. The question is, what will you decide to do with the tragedy and loss? Will it take you under? Will it make you stronger? Will it take you deeper? Will you allow it to take you to the next level?

Live the
DREAM

"Let patience have its perfect work, that you may be perfect and complete, lacking nothing" (James 1:4 NKJV).

JOURNAL
PROMPTS

- ❧ Has impatience ever gotten the best of you? How?
- ❧ What could you have done differently in that circumstance to be more patient?
- ❧ What adjustments have you made to be patient in similar circumstances?
- ❧ How has your own faith been tested?

Day 3

Embracing the Result

*I venture to suggest that the one vital quality which the great saints
had in common was spiritual receptivity. They differed
from the average person in that when they felt the inward
longing they did something about it. They acquired the lifelong habit
of spiritual response.*

A.W. Tozer

Behind the razor wire of a Florida State Penitentiary, a mother waits to visit her only son. Instead of allowing her own sorrow to completely engulf her, she looks around and notices the needs of the inmates' family members waiting with her.

Carol Kent, a professional speaker and author, is also the cofounder of a ministry she never guessed she would have imagined into existence. Speak Up for Hope is a nonprofit organization dedicated to supporting inmates and their families.

The journey began with a midnight phone call informing Carol and her husband, Gene, that their son, a graduate of the U.S. Naval Academy with an impeccable record and a strong Christian faith, had been arrested for the murder of his wife's first husband. Jason, the Kent's only child, feared for the safety of his two stepdaughters because their allegedly abusive biological father was seeking unsupervised visitation with the girls. Jason was charged with first-degree murder.

The Kents waited for two and a half years and through seven postpone-ments of their son's trial before he was convicted and sentenced to life in prison without the possibility of parole.

It's not the ending a mother wants or the story a Christian professional speaker and author wants to tell. But Carol trusts that God can bring good things from even the most terrible situations.

> I used to be what others would call "a professional." My masters degree is in communication arts, and I had worked as a public speaker and author for more than 15 years when my son was arrested. I was suddenly flat on my face, wondering if I would ever be able to speak publicly again. I wanted to curl up in the embryo position and die. My refining process has been to learn that when I am the weakest, He is strong. When we don't have answers, He is enough. When I can't pick myself up, He is "the lifter of my head." When tears come (and they often do), I don't have to pretend I don't hurt. I've discovered that God works better through my honesty, heartache, and brokenness than He ever worked through my professionalism.

Though her sorrow and circumstances are unwanted, Carol has allowed them to become a platform for ministry. "Not the ministry I wanted," she confesses, "but a richer, deeper ministry."

She has also cultivated the ability to recognize how small blessings in life reflect God's love for us on a daily basis, a skill that reminds us of His presence even when He seems to be absent.

> There are times when I'm driving home from the prison after visiting my son, and God reminds me of the joy I experienced as I ministered to the wife of an inmate at the prison that day...
>
> I have observed my son using his leadership, his education, and his faith to encourage other inmates and to make a differ-ence in the middle of a very dark and hopeless place. As I open letters from those inmates, telling me what an encouragement and blessing Jason has been to them, I feel the warmth of God's smile—and that makes my pain tolerable. I sense that

God is using my pain to give me a tender heart and to make me more useable. I don't like the process, but I embrace the result.[5]

What positive results of tough times can you see in your life? I am learning that if I don't come to a new level of self-awareness or understanding in the midst of pain, I miss the opportunity for personal growth. And even though the growth may be unwanted and uninvited, it's a sure means of developing full potential for a deeper and richer ministry.

In the stage play *Steel Magnolias,* one of the main characters, after suffering the death of her daughter, says, "That which does not kill us, makes us stronger." What she fails to add is, "only if we let it."

But it's not easy. The Refiner's fire is necessary to remove the impurities and produce a renewed strength and elegance in us (Psalm 66:10). But fire equals pain. And pain hurts. Sometimes it hurts so badly we miss what's waiting for us on the other side of the sorrow, heartache, and unhappiness. Instead, we walk gingerly through life so we don't have to feel anything too deeply or do much introspection.

But you can do it. You can get to the next level and live God's dream for you by discovering where you feel resistant in your life and then identifying what you can learn from it. Author Keri Wyatt Kent agrees:

> I believe our resistance, if we are willing to just look at it and hold it for a moment, will show us where we need healing in our lives. In my life, resistance shows me my fear, which is not always fun to think about...Often in life, when we feel pressure or resistance, we want to move away. Lean into the resistance; it will make you stronger. Don't run from your pain, and God will meet you in it and heal you.[6]

The idea of meeting God can generate fear or internal peace. Those courageous enough to meet Him in the midst of their circumstances, whatever they may be, have the guarantee of His provision. As Jesus did on the Mount of Olives before He was arrested, we can come before God and say, "Father, if you are willing, take this cup from me; yet not my will, *but yours* be done" (Luke 22:42). By surrendering, we show a willingness to grow through unwanted circumstances.

Carol Kent is extraordinary in that she's willing to embrace the result of tough times. Hers is an amazingly bold, mature, and courageous response—one that certainly challenges me to find the "embraceable" in my own difficult circumstances. Most of us often feel too overwhelmed during difficult times to begin the search for what we can yield.

Yet the moment we yield is the instant healing begins.

Live the
DREAM

Embracing the result of tough times will take you to a new and deeper level of healing and ministry.

JOURNAL
PROMPTS

- What circumstances are currently unwanted in your life?
- What's "embraceable" about these circumstances?
- What small blessings can you identify that have reflected God's love for you during tough times?

Day 4

Realizing God's Dream

*There may be another question that needs to be asked beyond
"What is God doing?" and that is this: "What is God dreaming?"*
ERWIN MCMANUS

God is not wasting the pain in your life. He never wastes a wound. He's healing you at this very moment and using that pain to show you a dream bigger than you realize.

Joni Eareckson Tada found her dream, but only after a diving accident left her a teenage quadriplegic. In a wheelchair for nearly 40 years, she's now a successful speaker, author, and artist, and a beloved advocate for the disabled. But coming to realize His dream has been a difficult journey filled with pain, patience, and healing. He calls you and me to the same journey.

Despite Joni's success, physical pain has shaken her faith many times. But she's learned to embrace the hope that does not disappoint because God promises us that if we stay obedient to Him, the product of suffering will be perseverance, character, and hope (Roman 5:3-5). "Hope," as Nouwen defines it, "is willing to leave unanswered questions unanswered and unknown futures unknown. Hope makes you see God's guiding hand not only in the gentle and pleasant moments but also in the shadows of disappointment and darkness."[7]

Notes Joni, "When I trust God in the midst of the most mind-bending pain, my hope is built up, not to mention my character." When we trust, we allow room for hope.

Trusting God to reveal His dream in our life and give us hope often requires an extraordinary act of willpower. When Joni wakes up and thinks, *Lord, I can't go on…I don't have the strength,* she refuses to let her emotions go down that dark and grim path toward depression. Instead, she prays, *Jesus, I don't have strength; but You do. I have no resources, but You do. I can't do this, but You can.* She says, "The weaker I am, the harder I have to lean on the Lord; and the harder I lean on Him, the stronger I discover Him to be. God *always* seems bigger to those who need Him most."[8]

This humbles me. *The harder I lean on Him, the stronger I discover Him to be.* When I'm in the dark, deep valley, I have to remind myself to hold on to the assurance that God never wastes a wound and that in my pain, I really do need to lean on Him.

Paul did. He was pounded by the evil one. All hell was against him. And in the dark valley, he cried out to God not just once but three times to get rid of the thorn in his flesh (2 Corinthians 12:7-8). It was really messing him up. But God chose not to take it away.

Paul realized something special in that moment, something God wants to show you and me as well—He's using our weakness to do His work in and through us, building trust, so that His dream for each of our lives can become a reality. We might paraphrase Paul as saying, "When I am weak and learn that He is there, He is present; I'm free, I'm strong" (2 Corinthians 12:9).

Did you ever do one of those "trust falls," where you fall backward into the arms of someone you trust to catch you? You give up total control and place absolute trust in that person to catch you in that moment.

God wants to teach you the same about Him—that you're not in control. He is. He wants to show you that when He seems most absent and you're falling backward, He really is most present and there to catch you. God walks beside you even when you can't see, hear, or feel Him. He provides you with what you need to get through deep pain, unbelievable circumstances, and surreal events. In your weakness, He wants you to place your hope in Him and let Him prove to you He will not disappoint.

But this requires you to step out in faith, and you must be willing to take the first step. Just like the Israelites for whom the waters of the river Jordan "piled up in a heap" when the priests carrying the ark of the Lord stepped into the water (Joshua 3:16), we too must step first, even when circumstances challenge our ability to do so.

Then provision comes. And again like the Israelites, we don't know what the provision will look like or how or when it will come. But it will. "Jesus says that maturity means growing willingness to be led—even to places we might not eagerly choose."[9]

More often than not, hardship blurs our vision of the future. And although much uncertainty lies ahead, you have to willingly take the first step, knowing that one thing is clear—you can be certain about who God is. Even with difficulties in life, He has overcome the world (John 16:33). So "be alert, be present. [God is] about to do something brand-new. It's bursting out! Don't you see it?" (Isaiah 43:19 MSG).

J.I. Packer explains that God has a purpose for our pain:

> This is what all the work of grace aims at—an even deeper knowledge of God, and an ever closer fellowship with Him. Grace is God drawing us sinners closer and closer to Him. How does God in grace prosecute this purpose? Not by shielding us from assault by the world, the flesh, and the devil, nor by protecting us from burdensome and frustrating circumstances, nor yet by shielding us from trouble created by our own temperament and psychology; but rather by exposing us to all these things, so as to overwhelm us with a sense of our own inadequacy, and to drive us to cling to Him more closely. This is the ultimate reason, from our standpoint, why God fills our lives with troubles and perplexities of one sort or another— it is to ensure that we shall learn to hold Him fast.[10]

We rarely understand how God is using pain in our lives to refine us. But just because we don't understand it doesn't mean He's not doing it. He is—because He has a dream for each of our lives.

Live the
DREAM

God uses adversity to help us realize His dream for our lives.

JOURNAL
PROMPTS

ɤ Have you ever leaned on God and discovered His strength as a result?

ɤ What scares you the most about taking the first step in adversity? How can you overcome that fear to walk in the hope that does not disappoint?

ɤ Write about a time in your life when your steps were slowed or uncertain. How did God walk beside you during this time?

Day 5

The Hands and Feet of Jesus

I want you to be concerned about your next door neighbor.
Do you know your next door neighbor?
MOTHER TERESA

Ask most women today what they would like to be. Needy? Dependent? Clingy? Certainly not! Independent? Self-sufficient? Survivor? Yes!

I was deeply moved recently by Carol Kent when she said, "I was used to being on the giving end of compassion, and I didn't like being needy. When I allowed the people closest to me to be the hands and feet of Jesus in the middle of my darkest hour, I experienced the comfort of being loved by Him."

Like Carol, we don't want to be needy. That's me. We're uncomfortable letting anyone know that all is not right in our world. We don't want to owe anyone. We worry about what people will think when they see the jumbled mess of emotions hiding just below the surface of our polished veneer. All of these reasons, plus a host of others, keep us from accepting the help that comes in response to tough times.

Help comes from unexpected places. A colleague who offers a tissue in response to unexpected tears. A neighbor you've never met who brings dinner over when she finds out your mother passed away. A friend who offers to keep your young children so you can fly out to your niece's funeral. Though all might not be Christians, all are Jesus' hands and feet in dark hours.

After her accident, Joni Eareckson Tada discovered that other people were her hands—literally. Unable to do anything for herself, she depended on others' hands to do the things she couldn't. Eventually, by taking things a day at a time and in bite-sized chunks, she learned to paint and write and drive with a joystick clamped to her arm. She acknowledges that before her accident she "couldn't have cared less about people like me." Now she finds joy in investing her time and energies in other people who are hurting.

Getting through tough times requires us to develop a new skill set. We may need to ask questions we've never considered or accept things that seem unacceptable. We may become sensitive to things we previously ignored. We might come face-to-face with ugly feelings we don't know what to do about. Our struggle may require difficult changes in current relationships or threatening changes within ourselves. In the midst of confusion and chaos, we might have to grab a lifeline that someone else offers. And when that happens, we have to decide to accept the help—a decision that is often unpleasant because of pride and an unwillingness to be beholden to anyone but ourselves.

Jesus reaches down from heaven through other people's hands, so when we refuse their help, we're actually refusing Him. We may have cried out for God's help, but when it comes in the form of another human, we're loathe to accept it. Why is that?

Pride often keeps us from letting others minister to us. Our need to be self-sufficient overpowers our willingness to accept help. We don't want to seem weak or needy. And yet when we're brave enough to accept help—and doing so does take courage—we'll discover, like Carol Kent, "the comfort of being loved by Him."

Getting through tough times includes another dimension. Rather than focusing solely on our own difficulties, we must also ask how we can help others walk through deep valleys. In addition to recognizing that other people are Jesus' hands and feet for us in tough times, we have to be willing to *be* Jesus' hands and feet for others. The gestures don't have to be expensive or grandiose. In fact, thoughtful and timely actions are more important. Small gestures take on big significance when one is hurting. When my father was ill, just a quick phone call or e-mail from a friend was often enough to get me through the day.

Statistics tell us that someone you know is grieving right now. How can you use your hands to reach out to her? I encourage you to call and check on her. Send a card or flowers. Prepare dinner. Invite her to spend time with you or simply sit and listen to all the conflicting emotions whirling around in her heart.

Support is often readily available in the first days after a major life change, so ask yourself how you can make a difference in a week, a month, or a year. Remembering the first anniversary of one's passing doesn't require more than jotting the date on your calendar, but the impact of the gesture is great. Families often dread the first-year mark, but their pain is lessened when they know others are marking it with them.

If you're in the midst of tough times yourself right now, how can you let others use their hands to be Jesus to you? Can you accept an offer of a meal? An offer of transportation? A willingness to run errands or grocery shop for you? An offer to cover your responsibilities so you can get out of the house? By saying yes, you'll let Jesus comfort you through the people He's placed specifically and purposefully in your life.

Let other people's hands embrace you in difficult times. Then, pass the love along through your own hands when someone else is in need. That's how God reaches down from heaven during tough times.

Live the
DREAM

In addition to recognizing that other people are Jesus' hands and feet for you in tough times, be willing to be Jesus' hands and feet for others.

JOURNAL
PROMPTS

- List examples of how other people have been Jesus' hands and feet in your life.
- Is accepting help from others difficult for you? If so, why?
- Whom do you know right now that you can walk alongside in a dark valley, and how can you best be Jesus' hands for them?

Week 8

Secrets to Finding Freedom

It is for freedom that Christ has set us free.
GALATIANS 5:1

How would you describe a person who is free—Content? Independent? Joyful? Loving? Alive? Passionate?

Do these words describe you?

How many women do you know who are really free? My hunch is not many. Bondage is everywhere. We're haunted by our pasts, burdened by self-pity, unwilling or unable to forgive ourselves or others, and held captive by our need to control. Instead of living big lives, we live small ones. Instead of living boldly, we live timidly. Instead of running freely, we limp along, dragging the leg irons we've clamped on our own legs.

That's not what Jesus wants for us.

A life with Christ is a life of possibility, of change, and of new beginnings. It's a life of hope and second chances. It's a life of freedom—but only if you choose to embrace the liberty He offers.

Jesus says, "Look at me. I stand at the door. I knock. If you hear me call and open the door, I'll come right in and sit down to supper with you" (Revelation 3:20 MSG). He wants to come into your heart to set you free. Will you let Him?

Being free begins by letting Christ in. Then we must be willing to identify our limitations and fears and agree to let go of them. We must be willing to own what's our responsibility and release what's not. We must be brutally honest with ourselves and the God who loves us. Once we've found freedom, we must be willing to hold on to it because the world and everything in it is against us and conspires to snatch it away.

Christ came so that you can be free. Are you living in freedom?

Day 1

The Power to Choose

We are always getting ready to live but never living.
RALPH WALDO EMERSON

My husband often quotes a famous line from the movie *Braveheart:* "Every man dies. Not every man really lives."

In spite of the fact that William Wallace lived under the corrupt English rule as a Scot and was martyred for his beliefs, he was a free man when he voiced these words. And even though he knew he was going to die, he refused to allow anything or anybody to determine how he was going to live.

Unfortunately, most people today are wrapped in bondage. Filled with anger and frustration, they live lives of resignation. Giving up much hope for their marriages, kids, and jobs, a *death of desire* has set in. It's what psychologists call "learned helplessness." In this phase, people literally come to believe they have no control over their lives and are locked into a system—family, government, job, institution, culture—and can't break free. They don't know how to change their circumstance, so they stop trying and instead become passive agents within the system. They make excuses for themselves and blame others because they believe they have no way out. A destructive cycle develops, draining the life right out of them.

Are you plagued by learned helplessness? Do you know somebody who is? It's a prison that many people never escape.

Viktor Frankl, a survivor of the Nazi death camps, wrote, "Everything can be taken away from a man but one thing: the last of the human free-doms—to choose one's attitude in any given set of circumstances, to choose one's own way."

That's inspiring. Even in the worst, most unimaginable circumstances, Frankl realized he could choose his attitude. It's the one thing nobody could take from him. It's one thing no one can take from you either.

But choosing your attitude is not easy. It comes with a price tag.

The path to freedom begins with realizing you always have a choice—even when you feel you don't. In the darkest times of life, when your options seem limited, you still have a choice.

You may be required to choose between bad and worse, but the choice is yours.

Often, you're able to choose between good and great. As long as you are willing to continue to exercise the freedom of choice, you will always have the opportunity to get better, be better, and do better in life.

Once you have learned that you have the power to choose, you must next recognize what is keeping you in bondage. Did you feel inadequate growing up? Does what you believe about yourself keep you from doing things you would love to do? Have you alienated yourself from others because you fear what they might think of you? Do you make decisions based on what others think? Once you realize what's imprisoning you, you then must choose how to release yourself from it.

Breaking dysfunctional patterns requires you to change your beliefs and behavior toward that which is enslaving you. You will have to consciously disconnect yourself from the systems you held dear by choosing to sever your connection between your attitude and that which enslaves you. To be truly free, something has to give.

Our heavenly Father understands. That's why He sent His only Son to die for you and me—so that we could experience true freedom. He showed His love for us in a way that we cannot ignore. Being free is choosing to embrace what Jesus did on the cross on our behalf and allowing our lives to be different as a result.

I don't know where the bondage in your life occurs. Are you captive to the past? Ashamed of what lurks in your personal history? Are you trapped by addiction, adultery, or debt? Do you require a full schedule or more things to make you feel alive? Does bitterness challenge your personal rela-tionships?

Only you and God know what you're currently wrestling with. But as Albert Einstein wisely observed, "We can't solve problems by using the same kind of thinking we used when we created them."

We take an essential first step toward true freedom when we become willing to accept the grace God freely offers us through Christ. Then we must be willing to *think* differently once we've accepted that grace. No longer do we depend on our own strength and abilities.

"It's an interesting thing, the human mind," say authors Bill and Kathy Peel in their book *Discover Your Destiny*. "It can only focus on a couple of things at a time. When we're preoccupied with a problem and focus on our own inadequacy to handle it, there's really no room to add God to the picture. The ability to think rationally returns only when we refocus on God's adequacy."[1]

God's adequacy helps us find freedom. If you're like me, however, you have a tendency to rely on your own sufficiency first and to turn to Him only when you're at the end of your rope. But we can't do that. It limits our freedom. Liz Curtis Higgs writes this about letting go:

> Jesus wants us to grow in faith, and we grow only when we come to the end of ourselves…That's when we must let go of the God of our own understanding. And embrace the God Who Is. Our neat and tidy God-in-a-box ideas about Jesus must be put aside as we seek after the real Christ, the one who won't fit in a tomb, who is both small enough to climb in our hearts and big enough to save the entire world.[2]

That's powerful! To see God for who He is, we need to get Him out of the box we put Him in and recognize the significance of our ability to choose. Choosing to walk in Him infinitely expands our potential.

Jesus is knocking at the door of your heart, but so is the world.

Live in freedom or live in fear. The choice is yours.

Live the
DREAM

To be truly free, something has to give.

JOURNAL
PROMPTS

❧ What internal connections to other beliefs or systems must die for you to be free?

❧ What choices do you need to take toward breaking free?

❧ How can you embrace the freedom Christ brings and live more boldly and bravely?

❧ How does God's adequacy affect your thoughts today? Do you believe He's adequate? Do you act as if He is?

Day 2

Worth the Wait

Patience is waiting. Not passively waiting—that is laziness. But to keep going when the going is hard and slow—that is patience.
UNKNOWN

Richard Swenson asks a searching question in his book *Margin:*

> What did we do with all our time before we had traffic lights, stalled interstates, telephones and busy signals, televisions, interruptions, junk mail, committee meetings, and cluttered desks? What did we do with our time before we spent it shopping for things we don't need?...Is it possible the time was used for things more inherently valuable than commuter traffic, busy telephones, and junk mail? Is it possible the time was used for conversing, for serving, for resting, for praying?[3]

No wonder we're so impatient. Time is a commodity, and we have to make the most of it. But are we? As the microwave generation—the generation who grew up on instant lunches and TV dinners, instant mashed potatoes, and now instant messaging—we believe the faster we get activities done, the more time we have for others.

But it never seems to work, does it? The faster we get things done, the more we cram, and the more we cram, the more we stress. Fuses get short, and we forget about God.

It's time to break free from the things that keep us captive, including our slavery to our self-imposed time frames. The Bible is clear: In his heart a man plans his course, but the LORD determines his steps (Proverbs 16:9).

As much as you and I would like to carefully map out our lives, God not only determines the *what* of our lives, He also influences the *when*. Because of this, we need to learn how to wait, which is tough work when living in a society where faster is better.

Karon Phillips Goodman addresses the waiting game in her book *You're Late Again, Lord: The Impatient Woman's Guide to God's Timing.* She notes a variety of reasons for waiting, one of which is self-development: "A great part of waiting purposefully is wrapped up in learning who I am so that I will know who I can become, the answers revealing themselves through each agonizing wait."[4]

Os Guinness, in his book *The Call,* writes that in order "to find out who you are, you must first find out who you're not." As you find out more about who you are and who you're becoming, you begin to see what you really need for God's dream to come true in your life. And as you allow God to paint the tapestry of your future, you will come to find that His timing really is worth waiting for.

But you must be willing to wait on the Lord. As Tim writes, "The problem is that we like shortcuts too much. We seem always to be willing to bypass the purity of the heart needed to develop and support purity of outward performance."[5]

Waiting patiently on the Lord isn't an easy thing to do. But by waiting on Him, we get the freedom of certainty. We're not certain of the outcome, but we're certain of who is overseeing the outcome. Charles Spurgeon said, "God is too good to be unkind. He is too wise to be confused. If I cannot trace His hand, I can always trust His heart." When we seek His counsel and wait until we have clarity, we have the freedom to move with confidence, either toward something that's good for us or away from something that isn't.

King David learned the value of patience:

- ❧ Wait for the LORD; be strong and take heart and wait for the LORD (Psalm 27:14).

- ❧ We wait in hope for the LORD; He is our help and our shield (Psalm 33:20).

- Be still before the LORD and wait patiently for Him; do not fret when men succeed in their ways, when they carry out their wicked schemes (Psalm 37:7).

- Wait for the LORD and keep his way. He will exalt you to inherit the land; when the wicked are cut off, you will see it (Psalm 37:34).

- I wait for you, O LORD; you will answer, O Lord my God (Psalm 38:15).

- I waited patiently for the LORD; he turned to me and heard my cry (Psalm 40:1).

Sometimes our waiting isn't just about self-development. Sometimes it's about preparation and readiness. "Finding yourself in your waiting room can be awfully confusing sometimes, especially when it feels as if you've done the right things or made the right decisions, and yet, you find yourself waiting. Don't be afraid—it just means that you're waiting for *something else* before you can move forward."[6]

Often we don't know what the "something else" is. But God does. He is an omniscient or all-knowing God who has searched you and known you. He knows when you sit and when you rise; He perceives your thoughts from afar. He discerns your going out and your lying down; He is familiar with all your ways. Before a word is on your tongue He knows it completely (Psalm 139:1-4).

The God who knows what you're going to say before the words leave your lips is the same One who knows the purpose for any waiting in your life. God has many reasons to let us wait, none of which we see until after the fact. For instance, God may want us to wait until...

- we gain more knowledge
- more favorable circumstances arise
- we have others' support
- financial provision is available
- we are emotionally prepared

We have a choice: Wait patiently and learn what we can in the process or wait impatiently and miss whatever refinement the delay holds for us. Author Cindy Crosby writes this about waiting: "God, what is this mystery?

That I wait, and you fill the waiting with something beautiful, yet previously unknown to me?"[7]

Waiting can reveal beauty. But most of us are too busy to look for it, or we don't really believe the beauty is going to be worth the wait. Some of us are simply afraid of the uncertainty. But beauty lies within uncertainty because with uncertainty comes possibility. And with possibility comes hope.

In order to experience the freedom Jesus came to bring, you must not resent the delays you experience in life. Though you might be able to make things happen in your own time frame, you often experience undesirable results when you take things into your own hands.

Pray as you wait. As you do, you'll discover the value of letting things come in God's time. You'll also find the beauty in waiting—the possibility that God's dream for your life is just on the other side.

Live the
DREAM

As you find out more of who you are and who you're becoming, you begin to see what you really need for God's dream to come true in your life.

JOURNAL
PROMPTS

- What are you waiting for in your life right now?
- What have you learned about yourself and God's provision in your times of waiting?
- What would "waiting patiently" look like in your life, and how might it be different from how you currently wait?

Day 3

Letting the Past Be the Past

Wisdom: to live in the present, plan for the future,
and profit from the past.
UNKNOWN

The past isn't the past if it's affecting your present.

What secrets do you harbor? Are you carrying around the heavy weight of shame? Are you dragging some baggage behind you?

Finding true freedom in Christ requires letting the past be the past. But many of us aren't able to do that. Though we know intellectually God in Christ has freed us, our memories haunt us, and we repeatedly pound ourselves for things we did. Some things we did years and years and years ago, and some things we did yesterday. All bind and burden us. Some we've kept to ourselves and pray that no one ever finds out. And some things we're ashamed that others already know.

Unresolved issues in your past form a yoke of slavery affecting your present, whether you realize it or not. We really are as sick as our secrets.

Whatever is holding you back, whatever is dragging you down, now is the time to let it go. You can learn from your mistakes and be disappointed you made them in the first place, but if you want to be free, you cannot keep pointing to them as evidence of your unworthiness or failure. That's not what God wants for you.

In her book *Radical Forgiveness,* author Julie Barnhill invites us to hold our secrets up to the light and to let them go: "Secrets hold their power only when they are hidden. Once placed in the light of God's love and revealed, they lose their power. Why not make today the day you clean those secrets out of your hidden closet? The day you refuse to give them power over your life anymore?"[8]

I'm not asking you to forget everything painful in your past. That's neither biblical nor beneficial. But I am challenging you to refuse to give those events power over your life anymore. "A mind filled with unresolved memories and unmet needs from the past is a mind clogged with pain, and it will cloud and pollute the truth it receives today."[9]

In choosing to find freedom, we must decide to release the power the past has over us. Perhaps your own pain comes from one or more of the following:

1. I had an abortion.
2. I was promiscuous.
3. I had an extramarital affair.
4. I stole from my employer.
5. I hit my children.
6. I lied on my income taxes.
7. I repeatedly disappointed my parents.
8. I dropped out of school.
9. I lost my job.
10. I _____.

I left the final blank so that you can add whatever it is from your past that haunts you.

Four steps will help you release the hold these activities have on you:

Acknowledge them. God already knows about them, but it's important that you come before Him and acknowledge your actions and your decision to release the hold they have on you.

Accept responsibility. This step is necessary even if you were reacting to circumstances beyond your control or to another person's behavior. Accepting responsibility requires being honest with yourself and God.

Make amends. If apologies are necessary, make them, but only if doing so doesn't hurt another person or reopen old wounds. You can sometimes push past the past without involving other people.

Forgive yourself. Our unwillingness to forgive ourselves often allows things from our past to resurface in the present. Previous bad judgments shake our confidence in making decisions today. Less-than-savory former activities lead to flashbacks, marring our ability to enjoy freedom in Christ now. This doesn't have to be. In the Bible, the word for forgiveness means "to abandon, send away, or leave alone." Forgiving ourselves means abandoning the memories of the past, choosing instead to focus on the present and the future.

You may still be caught up in some of the behaviors listed above. If you are, make the present your past before you hit rock bottom. Perhaps you've already made the plunge. Wherever you're at, make the choice now to turn it around before the bottom gets any lower. Ask God for His guidance, strength, and power as you release the hold these actions have on you. Remember Philippians 4:13: "I can do everything through Him who gives me strength."

As Tim writes, "True surrender begins in earnest very near the place where you hit bottom, but you enter this surrender with your eyes on Christ, not on what you surrender to Him."[10]

The things that hold us hostage keep us from enjoying a deeper, fuller relationship with Christ. Surrendering your past is not about dwelling on the things you did; it's about focusing on the One who looks beyond those things into your heart.

It's time to let the past be the past. Bring your secrets to the light and concentrate solely on the One who can heal you.

Live the
DREAM

The past isn't the past if it's affecting your present.

JOURNAL
PROMPTS

~ What baggage are you carrying around that you're ready to get rid of? (You may be more comfortable writing specific incidents on a separate piece of paper rather than in your journal. When you're done, burn the paper or shred it, signifying your willingness to abandon the hold these things have on you.)

~ Julie Barnhill writes, "Secrets hold their power only when they are hidden. Once placed in the light of God's love and revealed, they lose their power." Do you agree or disagree with her? Why?

~ How can you focus more fully on the One who looks beyond your past and into your heart?

Day 4

Letting Go

Faith, as Paul saw it, was a living, flaming thing leading to surrender and obedience to the commandments of Christ.
A.W. TOZER

What if you just let everything go?

I know you think that's a zany idea. An *impossible* idea. After all, people depend on you—your kids, your spouse, your boss. Perhaps your parents and some of your friends. Many in your church family as well.

Surrender everything? You may think that's crazy talk.

But crazy talk may actually be the opposite—not to surrender. Benjamin Franklin wrote, "The definition of insanity is doing the same thing over and over and expecting different results." Isn't that what we do? We constantly take control, doing things our own way, yet we're constantly left wondering what's wrong with what we're doing.

Surrendering is exactly what we must do. In fact, it's what God calls us to do—to place everything that's ours into His hands.

Many people mistake surrender for giving up. It's not. Writes Angela Thomas Guffey, "To surrender is to give up trying on your own. It is to have attempted life without God, or with only a casual acquaintance with Him, and found it unbearable, miserable, and shallow. To surrender is to know in your heart that you are not enough."[11]

Jesus invites us to surrender ourselves and everything we're responsible for into His sufficiency. In John 15:4-11, He gives us this instruction:

Remain in me, and I will remain in you. No branch can bear fruit by itself; it must remain in the vine. Neither can you bear fruit unless you remain in me.

I am the vine; you are the branches. If a man remains in me and I in him, he will bear much fruit; apart from me you can do nothing...If you remain in me and my words remain in you, ask whatever you wish, and it will be given you. This is to my Father's glory, that you bear much fruit, showing yourselves to be my disciples.

As the Father has loved me, so have I loved you. Now remain in my love. If you obey my commands, you will remain in my love, just as I have obeyed my Father's commands and remain in his love. I have told you this so that my joy may be in you and that your joy may be complete.

Jesus invites us to remain in Him so that His *joy may be in us and that our joy may be complete.* Surrendering leads to joy. Doris Leckey explains further: "Ultimately surrender is not about giving up, but about choosing life."[12]

Is letting go *and* choosing life really possible? Letting go seems to mean giving up on life. But that's just one of many paradoxes of the Christian faith. What at first appear to be mutually exclusive are actually intimately related. By giving up we gain, by releasing we secure, and by letting go we actually tighten our grip.

Surrendering can be a fearful thing. If we let go, will things fall apart? If we loosen our grip, will our children go astray? If we're not in control, whose hand will be on the steering wheel?

The truth is that we never have been in control. Believing we are is an illusion that's carried us through many years and many difficult times. Surrendering simply means recognizing and acknowledging the truth: Everything rests in God's hands, and leaving it there is best.

Surrendering does not mean giving up responsibility. You are still responsible to your family, your church, your job, and your financial commitments. Rather, it means you invite God to become even more intimately involved in your life. In doing so, you find freedom from the pressure to know it all, do it all, and be it all. Once the pressure is gone, we're able to fully blossom and be ourselves. As Leckey observes, "It's precisely in letting go, in entering into complete union with the Lord, in letting him take over, that we discover our true selves."[13]

What do you need to let go of? Control? Fear? Perfectionism? What other people will think? A difficult relationship?

Actually, God calls us to let go of it *all*—to place every last piece of our business in His hands and then to step back and watch Him do His amazing work. When we give our deepest desires and biggest concerns to God, He surprises us by making a way where none was apparent and by giving us energy to do our work with renewed zeal.

The more we surrender, the more we can accomplish. This is counterintuitive, but it's true. Jesus is blunt with us when He says, "Apart from me you can do nothing." In Matthew 19:26 He tells us, "With man this is impossible, but with God all things are possible."

So why not release everything to Him and draw on His power, His strength, and His wisdom? In doing so, you'll find freedom.

Live the
DREAM

Surrendering doesn't mean giving up. It means inviting God to become even more intimately involved in your life.

JOURNAL
PROMPTS

- Jesus invites us into His sufficiency. How does that idea strike you? More importantly, how will you respond to the invitation?
- If you struggle with the idea of surrendering everything to God, why?
- How can you invite God to become more intimately involved in your life?

Day 5

Reaching Out

Daughter, you took a risk of faith, and now you're healed and whole. Live well, live blessed! Be healed of your plague.
MARK 5:34 MSG

One of the most touching stories in the Bible is about a woman who hemorrhaged for twelve years. *Twelve years.* We know very little about her. We don't know her name. We don't know what caused her bleeding. We know nothing about her background.

I believe the lack of details is purposeful. Instead of judging her or her actions or comparing her illness to others', we can simply learn from her story.

> Then one of the synagogue rulers, named Jairus, came there. Seeing Jesus, he fell at his feet and pleaded earnestly with him, "My little daughter is dying. Please come and put your hands on her so that she will be healed and live." So Jesus went with him.
>
> A large crowd followed and pressed around him. And a woman was there who had been subject to bleeding for twelve years. She had suffered a great deal under the care of many doctors and had spent all she had, yet instead of getting better she grew worse (Mark 5:22-26).

Though we don't know her name or her circumstances, we do learn enough to feel sympathy. This woman had been hemorrhaging for twelve long years. Instead of being helped, she "suffered a great deal under the care of many doctors." If you've ever been ill and had to trudge from office to office, you know how wearing and disheartening it can be. Even more discouraging is that she "spent all she had."

A picture emerges: This woman is probably weak, frail, and anemic. She's desperate, penniless, and hopeless—until she hears about Jesus. Word has gotten around that Jesus specializes in tough cases: freeing a demon-possessed man, curing a leper, and raising a widow's only son. She's a tough case too, and she knows it. Could Jesus possibly free her too? She decides to take the chance that He will.

> When she heard about Jesus, she came up behind him in the crowd and touched his cloak, because she thought, "If I just touch his clothes, I will be healed." Immediately her bleeding stopped and she felt in her body that she was freed from her suffering (Mark 5:27-29).

Notice her hope in the face of hopelessness. That's who Jesus is: the Hope Giver. But He does more than give us hope; He also rewards our hope when we reach out to Him.

> At once Jesus realized that power had gone out from him. He turned around in the crowd and asked, "Who touched my clothes?"
>
> "You see the people crowding against you," his disciples answered, "and yet you can ask, 'Who touched me?'" (Mark 5:30-31).

I can just picture the disciples questioning Jesus. It was a madhouse. People were pushing and shoving, trying to get to Jesus. With so many people pressed so closely together, everybody was experiencing lots of unintentional touching. Yet something was different about this touch. As Liz Curtis Higgs writes, "There's a big difference between brushing against someone and touching them. One is accidental, the other is intentional. One is in passing, the other is on purpose. One might be rough, the other is almost certainly tender."[14]

Jesus noticed the tender touch because it caused the power to go out from Him. This wasn't just the touch of someone jostled in the crowd. It was the touch of a believer.

> But Jesus kept looking around to see who had done it. Then the woman, knowing what had happened to her, came and fell at his feet and, trembling with fear, told him the whole truth. He said to her, "Daughter, your faith has healed you. Go in peace and be freed from your suffering" (Mark 5:32-34).

I always squirm when I read this part of the story. Would I have the courage this unnamed woman shows? Would I really fess up to being the one who touched His clothes? This woman got what she wanted. Why didn't she just slink through the crowd and skedaddle when she could?

The answer is simple: Though she had been physically unclean for more than a decade, she never lost her truthfulness and integrity. She is frightened when she falls at Jesus' feet, but she tells Him the whole truth. Luke 8:47 tells us, "In the presence of all the people, she told why she had touched him and how she had been instantly healed." Though she is afraid, she becomes a ready evangelist, a living example of what reaching out to Christ will do.

Note what comes next: Jesus speaks to her. In those days, Rabbis did not speak to women in public. Jesus' action here is shocking. His words are even more shocking: "Daughter, your faith has healed you." Jesus not only healed her physically but also healed her emotionally by welcoming her into the family of God. Then He tells her that her faith healed her. Of course, His power had something to do with it! But Jesus credits her faith—her willingness to reach out to Him—as the reason she found freedom. He acknowledges what's happened, and then He speaks words of tenderness and encouragement to her. He says, "Go in peace and be freed from your suffering."

Jesus longs to speak the same words to you and me. Where you've been or what you've done doesn't matter. What matters is who He is. He's the Hope Giver and your ticket to freedom!

Live the
DREAM

*Jesus doesn't just give us hope; He also rewards our
hope when we reach out to Him.*

JOURNAL
PROMPTS

⚜ What touches you most about the story of the unnamed
hemorrhaging woman?

⚜ Would you have had the courage to admit touching Jesus'
clothes if you had been the woman in this story? Why or
why not?

⚜ Jesus says, "Go in peace and be freed from your suffering." In what area of your life do you need to apply these
words?

Week 9

Secrets to Creating an Intimate Relationship with God

What makes humility so desirable is the marvelous thing it does to us; it creates in us a capacity for the closest possible intimacy with God.

MONICA BALDWIN

When Tim and I were dating, we just couldn't get enough of each other, always looking for ways to be together. We were crazy, excited, on edge. We were stupid together—but too passionate to care what other people thought. Love does that to you. It can be so beautiful.

God desires the same thing with you. He created you for relationship and intimacy, and He wants *you* to feel crazy, excited, and on edge about Him. He is the "pursuer God," the One who never stops chasing you.

But most of us don't even realize He's pursuing intimacy with us. Or if we do, we may be afraid of it. If we have trouble with intimacy in earthly relationships where people have betrayed, hurt, or rejected us in some way, how can we develop intimacy with a God we can't even see? Many women live with this paradox—desiring intimacy with God but not sure how to be in such a relationship.

Look around you. How many women do you see in your office, church, community, or family living with such a reckless abandon for God they don't care what others think? What happened to passion, to people just burning to know Him and make Him known?

Many of us are experiencing a crisis of the heart. We often fear intimacy with God and others, and getting over this fear is virtually impossible. Being busy, overworked, and unable to unplug from our electronic society has suffocated the burning flame in our hearts. As a do-it-yourself society, filled with more luxuries than we can even use, we too often believe we only need God up to a certain point. We're like the father of the boy Jesus healed who confessed, "Lord, I do believe; help me overcome my unbelief!" (Mark 9:24). We believe Jesus for salvation, but we often fail to believe He can meet the needs of everyday life. Where we don't trust, we don't experience intimacy.

Only when you close this gap of unbelief and realize that "without Him you can do nothing" (John 15:5) do you open the door to true intimacy and begin a love affair with the lover of your soul. As Donald Miller writes, "I think the most important thing that happens within Christian spirituality is when a person falls in love with Jesus."[1]

Only then will the fire in your heart be glowing anew. I know it's not easy, but I want you to close the gap of unbelief in your life and find out what true love really does to you.

Day 1

You've Got Mail!

The Bible will keep you from sin,
or sin will keep you from the Bible.
DWIGHT L. MOODY

"Lose 20 pounds now and drop three dress sizes in two weeks!"

"Enhance your sex life overnight!"

"We'll buy your house for twice its value!"

Whether it's delivered to our mailbox or our inbox, we all dread getting junk mail filled with meaningless messages. But if I were to tell you about mail that could literally change your life, would you open it?

Only one mailing has a living, breathing message that can ignite your heart for life: the Bible. "Through the Word we are put together and shaped up for the tasks God has for us" (1 Timothy 3:17 MSG). Many of us do daily devotions or read books about the Christian faith, but most of these resources don't require us to actually open God's Word and read what it says.

Did you kind of just sink your shoulders when you realized I was talking about the Bible in this opening illustration? *Here we go again. Somebody pounding me to read my Bible.* If you did, I am with you. I know the feeling. Opening the Word takes work. I'll be the first to admit that to lie down and watch TV at the end of the day is easier. But I'll also tell you that fighting through the dread is the only way you're going to find the everlasting power of the Holy Spirit who will make you want to pick up the Bible every day.

How long has it been since you opened your Bible? As you read, do you take the time to reflect on what God is saying to you?

I am not asking these questions to make you feel guilty. The Lord knows we all have trouble staying on task. I ask the questions instead to challenge you about being in the Word on a regular basis.

Your mind-set has everything to do with whether or not you're reading it. Are you approaching the Bible with an attitude of drudgery, or do you see it as an adventure you can't wait to be a part of? We should come to God and His Word with a spirit of expectation. Here are some suggestions for making it an adventure.

Read it aloud. I know this isn't always possible (although other patrons at Starbuck's just *might* be interested in hearing you read Song of Solomon aloud!). Seriously, I experience the Bible in a different way when I actually form its words with my mouth and hear myself speak them. The very act of reading aloud—or hearing others do so—helps me truly listen to and comprehend the spoken message and notice things I may otherwise miss.

Practice deep listening. Sometimes we're so focused on the quantity of our reading that we don't really grasp the full meaning of the text. Keri Wyatt Kent addresses this issue in her book *Oxygen.* She suggests practicing deep listening, which requires us to read less but understand more. She instructs, "Read slowly, letting the words sink into your soul, listening for the one word or phrase that touches you most deeply."

As you read, notice the word or words that jump out at you. Jot them down or highlight them. After you're done reading, Kent suggests, spend time turning a word or phrase over in your mind. "What does God want to say to you? Is there some encouragement or challenge from Him in this word? What does He want you to know?"[2]

Deep listening requires extra work. But the benefit is worth the work because we can sense God's voice leading more clearly when we take the time to notice the words that resonate with us (or make us feel uncomfortable) and then figure out why they do. Deep listening helps us see new lessons in familiar stories in a way that other reading does not.

Personalize it. Placing your own name in Scripture brings out the power of the words. By doing so, you recognize God's provision and claim biblical promises for yourself.

For example, here's how Psalm 91:10-16 looks when I personalize it:

Then no harm will befall Julie,
  no disaster will come near her tent.

For he will command his angels concerning Julie
  to guard her in all her ways;

they will lift Julie up in their hands,
  so that she will not strike her foot against a stone.

Julie will tread upon the lion and the cobra;
  she will trample the great lion and the serpent.

"Because Julie loves me," says the Lord, "I will rescue her;
  I will protect her, for she acknowledges my name.

Julie will call upon me, and I will answer her;
  I will be with her in trouble,
  I will deliver her and honor her.

With long life will I satisfy her
  and show her my salvation."

Personalizing Scripture is a great way to banish fear, disillusionment, and hopelessness, as well as to remind yourself about the promises God has made to you.

Mix it up. Starting at the beginning of the Bible and reading straight through to the end can feel more like an obligation than an adventure. That's why you might consider mixing it up a bit. Start by choosing a book of the Bible you've always wanted to read. Find support materials that will help you understand the author and his background. Learn what you can about why he wrote the book and its context. Doing so will make your reading more meaningful and interesting. After you've finished this book of the Bible, pick another. Continue on until you've read through the entire Bible. Then start over!

Choose a customized Bible that meets your needs. Tim is the executive editor for *The Bible of Hope,* which includes themed articles, personality profiles, and key passages that address a wide variety of issues that challenge us today, including loneliness, abuse, marital communication, and forgiveness. Browse the Bible aisle in your local Christian bookstore or look online for a Bible that meets your specific needs. You'll find all kinds of Bibles, including one-year Bibles, devotional, chronological, and women's

Bibles, and one especially for new believers. One of these Bibles may be just what you need to breathe new life into your reading experience.

The word "intimacy" can be broken down and understood best as "into me see." To create intimacy with the God of the universe, you must see into Him. First, God sent Jesus. Then He sent you a love letter in the form of the Bible. The more familiar you are with Him and His Word, the more intimate the two of you will become.

Open it. Read it. Think about it. Pray over it. Embrace it. You've got mail every day. Go to your "inbox" and listen to what God is saying.

Live the
DREAM

*"[God's] word is a lamp to my feet and a
light for my path" (Psalm 119:105).*

JOURNAL
PROMPTS

- ✢ Practice reading a Bible passage aloud. Are you uncomfortable doing so? If so, why?
- ✢ Practice deep listening. Read Luke 13:10-17. As you read, notice which words resonate with you. What does God want to say to you through them? Pray for His guidance in understanding.
- ✢ If you're not currently reading the Bible on a regular basis, what can you do to incorporate this practice into your walk with the Lord?

Day 2

When Women Pray

The story of your life will be the story of prayer and
answers to prayer. The shower of answers to prayer will
continue to your dying hour.

O. HALLESBY

We've all asked the *why* question. You may be going through a period in your life right now where you're asking God why—or why not.

God, we need money, you cry out in desperation. *Why not help us?* Or maybe, *God, all I ever wanted is for someone to love me and grow old with. Why not now?* Have you ever wondered, *God, do you even care?*

Tired from the nagging fight, too many women become distressed and angry with God over the issue of prayer. Or instead of distressed and angry, they feel guilty because others around them seem to be praying so much more than they are. Whether they feel distress, anger, guilt, or shame, the bottom line is that God seems distant. But He is not.

He hears you and wants you to talk to Him. "Evening and morning and at noon I will pray, and cry aloud, and He shall hear my voice" (Psalm 55:17 NKJV). You cannot be intimate with someone you don't talk to. It's just that simple.

So how can we get over this nagging feeling that God is distant? How do we pray so that we connect intimately with our heavenly Father?

In his book *Whole Prayer,* Walter Wangerin identifies four parts of the circle of prayer, "First, we speak, while second, God listens. Third, God speaks, while fourth, we listen." Further, he observes, "We talk *with* God, not just *to* him. God talks with us, too, causing a circle to be whole and closed between us."[3] Focusing on all four aspects assures that our conversation with God is just that, a conversation that comes full circle.

Do you know somebody who doesn't know when to stop talking? Someone you avoid because if you start talking to her you may never get home in time to start dinner? Somebody who goes on and on, and when you finally have the chance to cut in and talk, you are forced to say "Well, I gotta run," only to repeat yourself again 20 minutes later? Think of the angst and frustration inside of you as you walk away feeling as though you were nothing more than a sounding board. Every time you see this person, you ready yourself for a one-way conversation.

I think too many of us do the same thing with God. We simply monologue by presenting our requests to Him, telling Him our worries and concerns about life, and maybe even thanking Him once in a while. But intimacy is about seeing into another person, and you can only see into somebody else by listening to what he or she has to say—a two-way conversation of give-and-take, talking and listening.

When we *really* listen, we're better able to hear God speaking to us by His Spirit, through the Bible, through friends, through circumstances, or through a gentle "knowing" that settles in our hearts. When He responds, we know His words will draw us closer to Him because whatever He asks of us is a reflection of His character. When we do more of what He wants, we become more like Him.

I want my children to understand this. My favorite times of the day are praying before school as I am driving with the kids and as I lie with them just before bedtime. On the morning drive, we talk to God; at night, lying quiet and still in bed, we listen. These are dynamic spiritual moments because the image I leave on their hearts as I kneel before the Father with them is what will carry them through life.

Slowing down to pray is difficult in our time-starved society, but we must do it. Getting alone and being still before God in prayer reinforces our dependence on Him.

When we get away from others and from our typical daily routine, we more easily recognize our total dependence on

God for our very existence. This realization can provoke some pretty stiff anxiety. But remember, it's this anxiety, this helplessness, and this vulnerability that expose our need and heighten our thirst for God; they compel us to seek refuge in His peaceful sanctuary. In contrast, people who constantly have the gas pedal to the floor are doomed to be godless.[4]

Prayer is about knowing God, not just knowing about Him. It's an ongoing discovery of the relationship we have with our Father through Jesus, and it's how we hear the beautiful things He wants to do in our lives.

Turning life into words to share with the Most High is not for the faint of heart. We need confidence to approach Him and faith that He will not disappoint us. Prayer is the vehicle by which we cement our connection with Him. It's the means by which we keep our relationship flourishing. Through it, we also begin to really understand ourselves and embrace who God made us to be. An active prayer life leads to an intimate relationship with God.

Here are some ways you can deepen your intimacy with Him:

Pray without ceasing (1 Thessalonians 5:17). God desires the continual prayers of His children. Over the kitchen sink. As you drive. When you tuck the children in. When you are alone.

Pray even when life doesn't feel right (Hebrews 4:16). The greatest deterrent to an active prayer life is the belief that everything in life has to be right or fixed before you can pray. Nothing could be further from the truth. God is simply waiting for you to reach out, just as you wait on the reach of your child.

Pray with faith (James 5:15). Come before God with a spirit of expectation. Nothing is wrong with believing God. He answers prayer, and He "is able to do immeasurably more than all we ask or imagine" (Ephesians 3:20).

Pray with thanksgiving in your heart (Philippians 4:4-6). Regardless of your circumstances, you always have something to be thankful for. When you offer praise and a heart of gratefulness to God, everything changes, even your anxieties. He knows your needs and promises to meet each one according to His riches in glory by Christ Jesus.

Prayer is your link to God. Pray often. Pray creatively. Pray genuinely.

Pray specifically. Then, listen. God speaks, but we must be still enough to hear Him.

When women pray, the whole world can change.

One prayer at a time.

One life at a time.

Live the
DREAM

An active prayer life leads to an intimate relationship with God.

JOURNAL
PROMPTS

- ❦ How can you make your prayers more of a dialogue (as opposed to a monologue)?
- ❦ Where is your favorite place to pray? Why?
- ❦ When has your prayer life been the strongest? How can you use this knowledge to reenergize your prayer life?

Day 3

An Obedient Heart

He is no fool who gives what he cannot keep,
to gain what he cannot lose.
Jim Elliot

Tim had to speak in Sunday school, and for once we were actually on time leaving for church. Peering out the window on the way to pick up my mother, I saw what looked like a dog running down the road. "Honey, look at that dog," I said to him.

"Oh no!" he replied, "I forgot to let She' Daisy in!"

She' Daisy is our dog, a chocolate Lab, and once again we were late for Sunday school. Letting She' Daisy in was the only thing I had asked him to do that morning, so you can imagine the special moment we had together as he dropped me off at my mother's and had me go back, in heels, to find that wonderful, adorable, and by now, filthy wanting-to-jump-all-over-me pet. I told She' Daisy it wasn't her fault, but Daddy's. She agreed.

As I look back on that day, I remember wondering whether She' Daisy was concerned about being let in or if she was embracing her newfound freedom. The dog I saw running down the road certainly seemed free. No cage. No owner to tell him to sit, shake, turn over, smile, or whatever else we have our pets do. She could roam wherever she wanted, do whatever she pleased, and cruise in anyone's yard she saw fit.

Or so it seemed.

Don't we live in much the same way? We think if we ignore or run away from our Owner's commands, we too can be free. Besides, God's commands can sometime seem burdensome. Don't get angry. Be careful with your tongue. Don't gossip. Be careful where you go. Avoid even the appearance of evil. Thou shalt not do this, thou shalt not do that. For many, being a Christian doesn't always appear all that exciting and fun. In fact, it's more on the boring and mundane side of life.

We often live as if we're on a Weight Watchers diet. We know our point allotment but add a few extra "brownie" (pun intended!) points. As long as things are going well in life, we "fudge" a little to add spice to life. But the more we self-indulge, giving ourselves over to sensuality...with a continual lust for more (Ephesians 4:19), the less sensitive we are to God's commands. We give ourselves over to our desires, our ways. Not His.

Eventually the dog that thought she was free began to feel the emptiness inside. To be fed she had to return to her owner. We, on the other hand, experience a deeper longing, the emptiness in our souls. The food that feeds the flesh cannot fill the soul.

Do we benefit when we give up our own control to run in the path of God's commands? The psalmist surely thought so. "I run in the path of your commands, for you have set my heart free" (Psalm 119:32).

Of course we want to live freely, but can we actually do that by following commands? I don't know about you, but I never *feel* free when I am being told what to do.

But that's precisely where we are wrong. As Erwin McManus writes, "Many of us are willing to settle for the feeling of being in control rather than making the choices that will genuinely give us freedom."[5] Too many often settle for what *feels* easier rather than doing what is actually right. The right thing and the easy thing are almost never the same.

King Saul learned this the hard way. God asked him to completely destroy Amalek, sparing not one thing, but Saul left behind sheep and oxen, among other things. When he tried to cover up his disobedience by telling Samuel his intention was to sacrifice the clean animals, Samuel reminded him that obedience is better than sacrifice, a common theme found throughout God's Word (1 Samuel 15:22; Psalm 40:6-8, 51:16; Proverbs 21:3; Matthew 12:7; Mark 12:33; Hebrews 10:8-9).

Saul willfully disobeyed the Lord because "he was afraid of the people and gave in to them" (1 Samuel 15:24). To obey God is to fear nothing but Him. Oswald Chambers writes about this:

> If we obey God it is going to cost other people more than it costs us, and that is where the sting comes in. *If we are in love with our Lord, obedience does not cost us anything,* it is a delight, but it costs those who do not love Him a good deal. If we obey God it will mean that other people's plans are upset, and they will gibe us with it—"You call this Christianity?" We can prevent the suffering; but if we are going to obey God, we must not prevent it, we must let the cost be paid.[6]

Doing what's right might cause others to be uncomfortable with your decision to obey. But we cannot worry about what others think of our decision. Even though "there is a way that seems right to a man...in the end it leads to death" (Proverbs 14:12; 16:25). Saul was eventually dethroned, and the Bible later says that "GOD was sorry he had ever made Saul king in the first place" (1 Samuel 15:35 MSG).

That knowledge scares me. I don't want God to ever regret putting me in a position where He's called me to serve. To truly "love life and see good days," we must obey our Creator (1 Peter 3:10).

When we do, intimacy flourishes with the One we obey. For "the eyes of the Lord are on the righteous, and His ears are attentive to their prayer" (1 Peter 3:12). God intimately hears those who listen to Him and do what He commands.

To be intimate, we must also be familiar with the one we're intimate with. God is already familiar with all our ways (Psalm 139:3); now it's time for us to become familiar with His. We're in brokenness and not intimate with God when we seek after our own desires (Ephesians 4:18), "But if Christ is in you, your body is dead because of sin, yet your spirit is alive because of righteousness" (Romans 8:10). You are His.

If you've run away from home, regardless of how filthy you are, your Father is at the doorstep waiting for you to return, arms wide open. Now follow and obey Him.

Live the
DREAM

Obedience sets your heart free.

JOURNAL
PROMPTS

- On a scale of one to ten, how sensitive are you to God's commands at this point in your life?
- Is God calling you to a step of obedience that you're resisting right now? If so, why are you resisting?
- Think of a time when you had to make a difficult decision between the right thing and the easy thing. What did you choose? Why? How did you process that decision?

Day 4

Divine Encounters

There are only two ways to live your life. One is as though nothing is a miracle. The other is as though everything is a miracle.
ALBERT EINSTEIN

Near the end of my dad's time on earth, as his physical strength ebbed and weakness crept in, he and my mother reported to Duke University Medical Center for him to be tested. It was early morning and the hospital was strangely quiet. Tired in their journey, they searched in vain for the lab they were to report to. Medicated heavily and starting to get really frustrated, my father was breaking down and wasn't strong enough to expend the energy to search the huge medical complex for his destination. As is often the case in hospitals, the many hallways and elevators made navigation confusing. They wound up in a deserted area of the hospital and could find no one to ask for directions.

Exhausted, my dad stopped in front of an elevator bank. My mom stopped next to him. Just then, a man appeared, encouraged them, and offered directions in response to my mom's query. They were to take the elevators before them. Relieved, my mom turned to push the button and then turned back around to thank the man for his assistance. No one was there. The hallway was deserted—and much too long for the man to have reached the end of it in the time it took to push the elevator button. Later they described the man to the nursing staff, who replied that no one fit that description. Not even close. My parents believe he was an angel sent by God.

Divine encounters like this are likely to surprise many of us, but those who know God and understand His ways are at peace about what happens in such moments. Here are two verses to remind you of how God loves to work in ways we can't even imagine. Pray over them—they're powerful.

> Do not forget to entertain strangers, for by so doing some people have entertained angels without knowing it (Hebrews 13:2).
>
> Are not all angels ministering spirits sent to serve those who will inherit salvation? (Hebrews 1:14).

I have no doubt that the man at Duke was a "ministering spirit" to my parents. They were heartened when they received the assistance they needed that morning at just the time they needed it. God seemed to reach down from heaven and assure them of His love during their struggle together.

Though some might see my parent's encounter with this mystery man as nothing more than unusual, my parents' faith enabled them to recognize it for what it was: a divine encounter.

I'm convinced that divine encounters are frequent occurrences in this world, yet they often go unrecognized. An intimate relationship with God increases our ability to see these encounters for what they are and heightens our awareness of their significance. Prayer, familiarity with Scripture, and obedience all develop our ability to recognize an encounter with God, whether through a "coincidence" or another person.

Though my parents' story highlights a goose-bump-inducing encounter, more mundane encounters also occur. And though they are more ordinary, they still have an impact. I've often been blessed by hearing song lyrics that addressed my fears and concerns at just the time they threatened to overwhelm me, or I've "randomly" opened my Bible to a verse that spoke to an issue I had been praying about. Sometimes my encounters come through repetition, hearing and seeing an issue of concern addressed by various people in various settings. None know that I'm struggling, but all "accidentally" offer timely advice.

God uses divine encounters to ease our earthly journey and provide clarity where confusion might otherwise exist. He designs them to assure us of God's presence and His interest in our lives. They remind us of His majesty and power, and they leave us breathless when they occur. They also help further the relationship with God that we so desperately crave.

As part of creating an intimate relationship with God, ask Him to help you recognize the divine encounters in your own life. They are there. Amazingly, the more you notice them, the more they seem to happen.

Live the
DREAM

Learn to recognize the divine encounters in your life.

JOURNAL
PROMPTS

- List the divine encounters you can think of in your own life.
- What message(s) do you believe God wanted to convey to you through these encounters?
- What can you do to develop your ability to recognize divine encounters?

Day 5

Getting to the End of Ourselves

*If we are not willing to wake up in the morning and
die to ourselves, perhaps we should ask ourselves whether or
not we are really following Jesus.*

Donald Miller

Have you ever been in a hurry to get somewhere, only to be stopped by a
detour sign that sends you in a direction you had no intention of going? I
have, and it drives me crazy.

By definition, a detour is a "roundabout way, a deviation from a direct
course of action."

I personally prefer to stay away from the deviations and instead take
the direct course. But as you and I both know, life's not that easy. It's filled
with detours.

Infertility. Education you have to put on hold. Illness. Taking care of
an aging loved one. Job loss. A long-held dream that's been sidetracked by
family issues. When these kinds of things happen, we might think God has
rerouted and forgotten us, leaving us on some abandoned stretch of road to
find our own way home.

As I look back over my own life, however, I see God's hand in each and
every detour. But I never found my way until I got to the end of myself.
We discover God's dreams for our lives only when we come to accept that
our lives are not our own.

Lysa TerKeurst thought she had her life all planned out. Then one ordinary day she and her daughters went to hear an a cappella choir of boys whose parents had died or disappeared during the civil war ravaging their Liberian country. Even while the choir toured the United States, their orphanage was attacked twice. As a result, all 12 choir boys faced homelessness until God revealed one of His dreams to Lysa.

While listening to the choir sing, Lysa…

> was overwhelmed with a sudden thought: two of the boys were meant to be hers. She literally put her fingers in her ears to drown out what she assumed was a divine message she didn't want to hear. At the postconcert reception, two boys named Mark and Jackson separated from the crowd, wrapped their arms around her, and called her mom. Fourteen-year-old Mark had a scar on his cheek from the hot poker of a rebel soldier; 15-year-old Jackson had hepatitis B, probably from contamination of a leg wound.[7]

Regardless, Lysa's family grew from three children to five as she decided to become the boys' mother.

Can you imagine Lysa approaching her husband to share the divine "knowing" that led to the boys' adoption? She remembers calling him from her cell phone, saying something like, "Do we need milk, and what would you think of adopting two teenage boys from Liberia?"

Once the couple decided to adopt, they arranged a cookout in their backyard to introduce the choir to their friends. As the boys sang, other hearts were touched. Unbelievably, all 12 eventually found new homes in the United States, as did many of their siblings, who had been left behind in Liberia. Now 15 families with 35 Liberian children are living in North Carolina, all because Lysa Terkeurst chose to obey God.

Genia Rogers also adopted one of the choir boys. The change in her family precipitated both a move to a new home and her return to work in order to address the financial reality of adding a third child to her brood. Despite the changes, she notes, "All the blessings of my life have come from stepping over a precipice when I could have what-if'd myself out of a decision."[8]

Getting somewhere without a detour is the easy way, but we learn few (if any) lessons when the path is clear. Discovering God's dream for your life is much the same way. It's usually never the easy road, but the emotional and spiritual growth is priceless.

Though detours are often inconvenient, when we finally get to the end of ourselves, we sometimes discover that they're actually full of delightful surprises. As we journey along paths we wouldn't have otherwise taken, God's dreams for our lives often become clear. Lysa, Genia, and countless others who decided to empty themselves for the sake of others find they've been blessed as a result of their detours.

When life doesn't go as you plan, the challenge will either hurt your relationship with God or it will deepen it. The difference lies in your response to the challenge. Will you be able to overcome the anger and uncertainty you feel when you're forced to respond? Or will it take you under? You cannot resent the changes that come in life without doing damage to yourself; that selfishness will eventually tear you down. Instead, you must embrace the mystery of what God has in store for you. Though it's not a natural act, you must change your question from *Why me?* to *What can I learn?* and *What is God doing?*

As Erwin McManus writes, "While we strive to fill ourselves and remain empty, Jesus emptied Himself and lived fully."[9]

If you want to discover God's dream for your life, you must come to the end of yourself. For "whoever finds his life will lose it, and whoever loses his life for My sake will find it" (Matthew 10:39).

Surrender to the detours He's planned for you. They lead to the end of yourself and to the true beginning of your intimacy with Him.

How will you respond?

Live the
DREAM

Accept that your life is not your own. It's His.

JOURNAL
PROMPTS

⚜ Are you currently experiencing a detour? If so, what are you learning from it?

⚜ If you look hard enough, can you see God's hand in this detour?

⚜ Genia Rogers said, "All the blessings of my life have come from stepping over a precipice when I could have what-if'd myself out of a decision." Do you need to step over a precipice?

Week 10

Secrets to Making Every Day Count

Whoso loves, believes the impossible.
ELIZABETH BARRETT BROWNING

"Just one game of baseball. Ask God that I will get to watch little Zach play just one game of baseball."

That's what my dad whispered in my ear at Greenville Memorial Hospital as he was broken with pain and filled with a cancer that would too quickly take his life. It was all I could do to keep from collapsing myself. He never did get to see Zach play. But in so many ways he did, and now I know he does from a heavenly vantage point.

In our early years of marriage, I remember Tim preaching from James 4:14 (NASB) that life is but "a vapor that appears for a little while and then vanishes away." The message had become real to him when he was 16 and a younger sister suffered a traumatic head injury from a car crash. God got his attention, and he is now committed to living life to the max and embracing every minute. The older I get, the more I too understand how brief life is. More importantly, I am learning that life is best lived one day and one decision at a time.

Because our time on earth is limited, none of us know how many days we have left. But the number of days is far less important than how we spend them.

I know of a woman whose life mission statement is to love the Lord her God with all her heart, mind, and soul and to love her neighbor as herself (Matthew 22:37-39). That's quite a mission and certainly not easy to do! But it reminds her to live every day beyond herself, whether she feels like it or not. A mission statement is a great place to start.

Elizabeth Barrett Browning said that "whoso loves, believes the impossible."

When you love, you're bold, fearless, and courageous—all things necessary to making every day count.

Day 1

To Know Him and Make Him Known

*I will greatly rejoice in the LORD, my soul shall be joyful in my
God; for he has clothed me with the garments of salvation,
he has covered me with the robe of righteousness,
as a bridegroom decks himself with ornaments,
and as a bride adorns herself with her jewels.*
ISAIAH 61:10 NKJV

I remember when Zach (about age seven at the time) came busting into the house screaming, "I saved him, I saved him!" referring to his little buddy he had been witnessing to about Jesus. "Yes sir," he told his dad, "I told him about Jesus, and he prayed for Jesus to come into his heart. I saved him, and I hope he lives different now." I smiled.

Have you ever wondered why we make the "living different" part so complicated? Maybe it's because change is so hard. Not salvation—that's by grace...a gift from God. The change part is the hard part.

Kim is a new believer. Her enthusiasm for Christ is contagious, but she secretly grieves her past and all the unwise decisions she made. Instead of shedding these burdens, she carries them around, partially as penance and partially as a reminder not to repeat these mistakes again. But carrying around such a load is pointless, even crippling. Because "if anyone is in

Christ, he is a new creation; old things have passed away; behold, all things have become new" (2 Corinthians 5:17 NKJV).

Though Kim is making faith-based decisions now, she struggles to believe she's a new creation. She wonders, *How can I possibly become new when my past is so tarnished?*

This one question haunts so many. One of the devil's ways of making you doubt the saving power of Christ Himself is to make you think God couldn't possibly forgive and wipe clean all the stuff you did. If to love is to believe the impossible, then to love Christ is to believe that "what is impossible with men is possible with God" (Luke 18:27).

To forgive ourselves for the mistakes we've made, we need the same assurance Paul had, "being confident of this very thing, that He who has begun a good work in you will complete it until the day of Jesus Christ" (Philippians 1:6 NKJV).

Life as a Christian is a progression. We don't just suddenly have the ability to do better, be better, and make wiser decisions. Neither is everything all hunky-dory in the Christian life. In fact, things tend to get even harder. But as we invite Christ into our lives and learn about His nature, we begin to change in response to the knowledge that He really is involved in the process of sanctifying us (1 Thessalonians 5:23). The more we know about Him and the more we experience His presence and unfailing love for us, the more we are able to move boldly and confidently into the world, believing that with God all things really are possible.

Though our salvation is guaranteed the moment we accept Jesus Christ as our Lord and Savior, the transformational work in us continues. This means two things: You're both new *and* a work in progress.

Kim is a new creation in Christ and needs to let go of the baggage from her past that's weighing her down. You may need to do so too. Then you'll be more likely to take the next step God calls you to as a new creation: to "let your conduct be worthy of the gospel of Christ" (Philippians 1:27 NKJV).

Making a decision to be a Christ follower is one thing, but living that way day in and day out is quite another. This is where we all have difficulty.

Instead of focusing on what we're doing right in our walk with God, we focus on our shortcomings. Instead of focusing on how far we've come, we focus on how far we have to go. Instead of encouraging us, our focus discourages us. Instead of looking ahead, we look back. And like Kim, many don't like what they see.

Transformation requires spending less time dwelling on the past and focusing more on who you're becoming. The evil one would have you look back with regret; God would have you look forward to His kingdom.

I remember a story A.W. Tozer tells in a booklet called *Total Commitment to Christ:*

"One time a young man came to an old saint...and said to him, 'Father, what does it mean to be crucified?'

"The sage replied, 'Well, to be crucified means three things. First, the man who is crucified is facing only one direction.'"

Tozer explains, "If he hears anything behind him he can't turn around to see what's going on. He has stopped looking back...[and now looks] in only one direction...the direction of God and Christ and the Holy Ghost."

"The sage continued, 'Another thing about a man on a cross, son—he's not going back.'"

Tozer again expounds on the man's wisdom: "Get a man [or woman] converted who knows that if he joins Jesus Christ he's finished, and that while he's going to come up and live anew, as far as the world's concerned he is not going back—then you have a real Christian indeed."

"Finally the old sage finished, 'One thing more, son, about the man on the cross: he has no further plans of his own.'"[1]

To be crucified with Christ means you're facing one direction. You cannot turn around. And because you no longer live, but Christ lives in you, your own plans must go (Galatians 2:20). Such focus leaves no time for regret.

God has a dream for you. He sent Jesus so that you "can have real and eternal life, more and better life than [you] ever dreamed of" (John 10:10 MSG).

Do you know Jesus Christ as your personal Lord and Savior? If not, I encourage you to pray the following prayer to accept Him into your heart. It's the first step to making every day count.

> Father, I know I have sinned against You, and I'm sorry. I am now ready to turn away from my sinful past and become a new creation in You. Please forgive me of my sins and begin Your work in me. I believe that Your Son, Jesus Christ, died

for my sins, was resurrected from the dead, is alive, and hears my prayer even now. I invite Jesus to become the Lord of my life and to rule and reign in my heart. Please send Your Holy Spirit to help me obey You and to do Your will for the rest of my life. In Jesus' name I pray. Amen.

You are now a new creation, born again to know Him and make Him known. Love Him, love others, and let others know about Him.

Live the
DREAM

*As a new creation you are washed clean.
It is no longer you who live, but Christ lives
in you (Galatians 2:20).*

JOURNAL
PROMPTS

- ⚜ What does becoming a "new creation" mean to you, and how does this knowledge change your view of yourself?
- ⚜ How do you feel knowing that "He who began a good work in you will carry it on to completion until the day of Christ Jesus"?
- ⚜ A friendship with Jesus guarantees peace, companionship, acceptance, and forgiveness. Are you actively embracing these things in your life? If not, how can you begin?

Day 2

What Matters Most

Tell me who you love and I will tell you who you are.
ARSÈNE HOUSSAYE

I sat in my car the other day after I had taken the kids to school, and my mind began racing as I realized that my little girl is growing up way too fast. This is hard on a mom. She'll be a senior next year and then off to college. She says she can't wait to move into the dorm with her best friend.

I remember how exciting it was to go off to school. I couldn't wait either! And I want that for her, I just can't believe how quickly she has grown up. Now she's driving and boys are calling, and...

The phone rang.

Tim was calling me just as I was in the middle of all this. As I started to talk with him, he could tell I was a mess. We talked and celebrated in that moment all that God has given us, our children in particular. We pray we've given them the foundation they need to develop strong relationships when we launch them on their own.

How well you live hinges entirely on your ability to develop healthy relationships with others. Your relationship style is one way of understanding how you do and don't do relationships. Tim writes,

> A person's style is a mental model...of basic assumptions, conclusions, or core beliefs about one's self and others. The first

set of core beliefs, or relationship rules, [is how you view] *self.*
It centers around two critical questions:

1. Am I worthy of being loved?
2. Am I able to do what I need to do to get the love I
   need?

The second set of beliefs forms the *other* dimension. It centers
around two other important questions:

1. Are other people reliable and trustworthy?
2. Are people accessible and willing to respond to me when
   I need them?

Your sense of *self* as well as your sense of *other* is either positive
or negative based on your answer to these four questions.[2]

If you answered yes to the four questions, you most likely feel safe and
content in close relationships, even when there's conflict. If you answered
one or more questions with a no, that's when discontent creeps in. When it
does, we immediately try to stop the pain.

> Emptiness seeks fullness. Brokenness longs for wholeness.
> Exhaustion seeks restoration. In pain, confusion, anger, and
> alienation, we begin to search for *anything* to make our pain
> go away—even if only for a brief moment. We're desperate to
> slake our thirst, even if every swallow moves us closer to the
> end.[3]

In looking for the *anything* to make our pain go away, we often end up
with "disordered affections," which occur when we rely on things other
than God to fill the holes in our hearts—food, alcohol, an affair, por-
nography, drug use and abuse, shopping, gambling, exercise, or even an
obsession with a hobby. Instead of looking to God and the relationships
He's placed in our lives, we look to other things to fill the emptiness and
ease the confusion we feel.

Admitting we've begun to fill our internal emptiness with things other
than God isn't easy. Instead of being our first defense, He's often our last.
That's when we get into trouble.

The secret to making every day count is to focus on what matters most.
This is incredibly difficult to do in a world that values wealth, beauty, and

fame. The decision to focus on our relationships—with God and others—is directly at odds with what society values. We can't aggressively pursue wealth and assume our relationships will remain intact. We can't focus on beauty first without signaling to others that what's on their outsides is more important than what's on their insides. And we can't pursue fame without giving up valuable amounts of privacy in our relationships.

If you first agree that relationships with God and others are what matter most, the next important step is to ask yourself what you're doing to further your relationships. Often, we're so caught up in life that we inadvertently put our connections with others on autopilot, hoping that the relationships will still be intact when life settles down a bit. Because life rarely settles down, we can go weeks, months, and even years without investing time in the people we love most.

Yet our investment in others can set them free. And us.

> Think of the husband who comes home tired and dejected after a rough day at work. The fire that fuels his competitive edge at the office is nearly snuffed out. Then his wife, who has worked a full day herself says, "I understand, baby. You're still the man!" She hugs him and says, "I love you, no matter what." Is it any wonder that he goes to work early the next day, ready to charge hell with a water pistol? He is loved, so the obstacles just don't matter. It's hard to beat a man who knows he's already won.[4]

Where your treasure is, there your heart will be also (Matthew 6:21). Where is your heart? Is it trapped by the human desire to store up treasure in this world (in the form of an impressive work title or job, a high income, an expensive home, a nice car, awards, and recognition)? Or do you focus on people the way Jesus did when He was here on earth?

What matters most? It's a question each of us must answer. And the sooner, the better.

Live the
DREAM

Set your heart on your relationships with
God and with those you hold dear.

JOURNAL
PROMPTS

- Where is your treasure?
- How are you influenced by society's emphasis on wealth, beauty, and fame?
- In your current relationships, what's keeping you from going deeper or growing closer to each person—their "stuff" or yours? If it's yours (or partly yours), what can you do about it?

Day 3

Making a Difference

There are five Gospels of Jesus Christ—Matthew, Mark, Luke, John,
and you, the Christian. Most people never read the first four.
Gipsy Smith

You had an influence today for good and/or bad with your children, husband, friends, and more.

If I had the chance to talk to those you love, those you work with, those who look up to you, what would they say? "All she does is yell. She's angry all the time. Stressed. Preoccupied. She doesn't care about me."

Or would they say, "I love being with her. I can talk to her. I wish she was with me right now…"

I hate being on the receiving end of someone else's "stuff." It's belittling and discouraging. That's why—come rain, wind, bad traffic when we're late, or spilled cereal in the car—I make a careful choice of how I respond to my kids. I know my behavior affects how they walk into school for the day. Sometimes I have to calm down and pray first and then reorder our world. But it's important to me that they hear love in my voice, not anger and frustration.

If you haven't seen the movie *It's a Wonderful Life*, it's worth your time. George Bailey runs a modest building and loan company in the town of Bedford Falls. When financial trouble besets the company, George thinks his loved ones would be better off without him and contemplates ending his life. Thanks to a gentle angel named Clarence, however, he gets a glimpse of what Bedford Falls would be like without him in the future and realizes, for the first time, how his own humble life has influenced more people than he knows. The glimpse encourages him to choose life—thereby continuing his positive influence on the community.

Like George Bailey, our influence extends well beyond what we suspect. As we touch others, they in turn pass it on. Positive influence, like a good virus, is contagious. Kind deeds lead to other benevolence. Good advice gets passed along. An encouraging smile spreads from one person to another. A comforting hug is later shared.

We cannot adequately measure our influence. Perhaps God intended it that way to keep us humble. Often, the people we touch don't realize it until years later.

Abraham Lincoln credits his mother, Nancy Hanks, who died when Lincoln was only ten, as being chiefly responsible for all he was or ever hoped to become. Thomas Edison, whose teachers felt he was "addled" and slow, was educated at home by his mother. He later said, "My mother was the making of me. She was so true, so sure of me; and I felt that I had someone to live for, someone I must not disappoint."[5]

You do not need to be a biological mother to have influence on another person's life. Most people can name the teachers who had the biggest impact on them. Others name mentors or older women. Some rely on sisters, aunts, or grandmothers. Regardless of the tie, what matters most is that you are willing to make every day count by investing in the life of another human being.

Take a minute to list those you currently are (or could be) influencing. Then ask yourself if you're being intentional and deliberate about this influence. Search your heart to determine what you're willing to invest in those on your list (time, money, experience, contacts, and other resources). Then make a plan to increase your influence in the lives you can realistically touch. Your investment in other people is the only thing that will outlast you.

Phil Vischer was the visionary behind the creation of *Veggie Tales*, the animated video series featuring a cucumber named Larry and a tomato named Bob, and the founder of the company responsible for the duo, Big Idea. Together, Bob and Larry influenced an entire generation of young people by teaching them biblical virtues through an assortment of vegetable characters. Though millions of children can sing the *Veggie Tales* theme song, Vischer no longer owns Big Idea. After expanding too quickly, the company was forced into bankruptcy. Vischer writes about the experience in his tome, *Me, Myself, and Bob,* which is part memoir and part business tutorial.

At the end of the book, Vischer outlines the lessons he learned from the rise and fall of Big Idea.

> The world learns about God not by watching Christian movies, but by watching *Christians.* We are God's representatives on earth—his "royal priesthood." We are his hands and feet. What I put in my movies is more or less irrelevant if it isn't coming out in my life. I realized I had become so busy trying to "save the world" with my visionary ministry that I was often too stressed and preoccupied to make eye contact with the girl bagging my groceries at the supermarket. And where does Christianity actually happen? Where does the "rubber meet the road," as it were? Up on the big screen in a movie theater? On TV? No. Across the checkout line at the grocery store, between me and a girl who makes a fraction of what I make and assumes I don't give a rip about her life. That's where it matters. And that's where, I realized, I was blowing it every day…On my next trip to the grocery store, I made a point to smile at the checkout clerk and ask how she was doing. I meant it too.[6]

Like Vischer, we must understand where the "rubber meets the road" and strive to live in that place. You are the hands and feet of Christ, and others are influenced in their own walk with Him by watching you live out yours. To live in a way that lifts up Jesus and honors God is a mighty big calling, but it's something we must do every day.

What message are you sending to the girl behind the counter at the supermarket? To your children? To your coworkers?

The question isn't whether you are making a difference. That's a given. The question is, what kind of difference are you making?

Live the
DREAM

*Make every day count by investing in the
life of another human being.*

JOURNAL
PROMPTS

- Who has influenced you in your life? What are you doing to pass this influence along?

- What's one thing you can do today to be a positive influence on another person?

- Where does the rubber meet the road in your life, and how does that influence the choices you make?

Day 4

Savoring Motherhood

It's not only children who grow. Parents do too. As much as we watch to see what our children do with their lives, they are watching us to see what we do with ours. I can't tell my children to reach for the sun. All I can do is reach for it myself.

JOYCE MAYNARD

The power is undeniable, the bond virtually unbreakable. Few would ever deny the influence and authority that comes in one small word: "mother." In any language its meaning holds universal acclaim, affection, and admiration.

The older I get, the more I come to love and appreciate my mother. Tim's mother, who died far too young more than ten years ago, was also a godly and powerful influence in our lives. Those of you with godly mothers are blessed.

The search for lost fathers is on, but special thanks should go to moms everywhere for being there for their children and for giving of themselves. Mothering does matter—don't let anyone tell you otherwise. Nothing in life can compete with a mom's warm embrace and loving devotion. Who else would wipe those snotty noses and gently kiss feverish foreheads goodnight? Nothing is more important than the investment you make in a child's life.

We had a lot of fun growing up, going on vacations, visiting my grandparents in North Dakota, and more. But when I think about my mother, I don't think about the things we did. I think about her. When I think about the wonderful times we had with Tim's mother for holidays and gatherings, I don't focus on them, I think about her. This points us to an important truth. We talk a lot about making memories, but that's not really what matters. You don't make memories. You are the memory. It's not about the trip you took to Disney World last year with your children. It's not about the time you took them to the beach and rode the 100-foot-waterslide, scared to death and trying to keep your makeup intact. And it's not even about taking them to church every Sunday. All of those are important, and I don't want to minimize them, but what your kids really want and need is heavy doses of *you*. God made it that way.

Ephesians 5:15-16 (NKJV) gives us a strong warning: "See then that you walk circumspectly, not as fools but as wise, *redeeming the time*, because the days are evil." Paul knew about the everyday distractions that hinder our relationships with God. The same is true in our relationships with our children.

What obstacles are stealing away your time from your children? The phone, the Internet, busyness? Make a vow to set aside those obstacles and invest your time building lasting and healthy relationships. Redeem the time God has given you—use it to your best. Put God first and family second, and the rest will fall into place. Why? No one will love your children as much as you do. He has loaned them to you so He can work through you to make them more like Him.

In the end, what really matters in life? Is it the deadline at work or the little league ball game or ballet recital you promised to attend? Is it the business trip across the country or being there when your husband is facing tough times?

Tim and I have made many relational sacrifices in the past, but now we more often delay work projects and postpone business trips just to spend time with each other and our children. Looking back, we can honestly say this has never caused us loss. On the contrary, we have gained numerous wonderful and rewarding times together. These moments are the "timeless" treasures we can take with us through life. The Word says that if you don't take care of your family, you are worse than an infidel (1 Timothy 5:8). That's a pretty strong word.

The Bible says children are a heritage from the Lord, a special gift. They are on loan from God, given to us for only a season. As parents, our primary, God-given responsibility is to help our kids become more like Him. And we can do that when we give our kids a healthy, godly love.

So tonight when you tuck your daughter in bed, or gaze at that young man across the dinner table, be sure to take a second look. Touch her face as she sleeps. Kiss his forehead. Squeeze her hand. Join us in praying, "Father, the day is coming when my kids will be grown up and gone. Please give me the wisdom and strength to love my kids as You love me. Thank You for loving me with an everlasting and perfect love, in Jesus' name. Amen."[7]

Live the
DREAM

In the end all that matter are the relationships in your life and how you invest in them.

JOURNAL
PROMPTS

- How can you redeem the time?
- What traditions, occasions, or special times do you currently have with your children and/or family? What can you begin doing to be a memory in the lives of those who love you?
- Whom do you remember most? Why do you remember that person? Are you that kind of person in someone else's life?

Day 5

Enough

We were born to make manifest the glory of God that is
within us. It's not just in some of us; it's in all of us. And when
we let our own light shine, we unconsciously give other people
permission to do the same. As we are liberated from our
own fear, our presence automatically liberates others.

NELSON MANDELA

What is life really all about?

I think of Jeremiah 17:9, where the prophet says, "The heart is deceitful above all things and beyond cure. Who can understand it?" We walk through life as if it all revolves around us, fussing and worrying about so many meaningless things. Just think about some of the arguments you've had with others—drama that really amounted to nothing but apologies if you were lucky and broken relationships if you weren't.

As Christians we should live differently. But we usually don't.

Consider George Barna's research. He found that the divorce rate is higher among Christians than non-Christians, and more non-Christians than Christians give to homeless and nonprofit organizations. Both groups reported being equally satisfied with their lives. Barna concluded that "[Christians] think and behave no differently from anyone else."[8]

This truly saddens me because as women of God we are called to live "holy" lives—set apart from the rest of the world. J.I. Packer, in his classic work *Knowing God,* writes, "When one sees…randomness and immaturity in Christians, one cannot but wonder whether they have learned the health-giving habit of dwelling on the abiding security of true children of God."[9]

Are you dwelling on the abiding security of being a true child of God?

It's difficult. We have highlighted how so much interferes with this security and the pursuit of holiness. Other people. Deadlines. Expectations. Work demands. Making a living. Life becomes difficult when we try to divide our time and attention evenly and fairly among it all. But you can manage it, and you can be set apart by understanding this one principle: *God is enough.*

Please don't skip over what you just read. You'll be tempted to because it's probably something you hear time and time again from well-meaning Christians. Unfortunately, though, repetition can make us immune to the message.

To become an extraordinary woman, you need to catch this. Once you understand it and apply it to your life, you suddenly see yourself moving from the ordinary to the extraordinary, from the mundane to the unimaginable, and from the uncertain to the certain. You don't blend in anymore because you now live differently. It's no longer about *you.*

When things are falling apart around you, God is enough. When illness invades your life or that of a loved one, God is enough. When you feel you goofed up or lost your way, God is enough. When life is out of control, God is enough.

Focusing on God's sufficiency is the most important step toward capturing God's dream for you. But remember this: The journey isn't about capturing the dream. *The journey is about knowing the God who placed the dream in you to begin with.* If you focus on the dream and not God, your focus is misplaced, and you'll get lost and stumble. But if you focus on God first, He'll provide what you need to grasp the dream.

I believe we're often just like Elijah in 1 Kings 19: We're only looking for God in the big things in life. Because of that, we miss Him in the little things. Brent Curtis and John Eldredge note, "God is not 'out there somewhere' in some dramatic way, waiting to commune with us by earthquake or fire or signs in the sky. Instead, he desires to talk with us in the quietness of our own heart through his Spirit, who is in us."[10]

Are you listening to what God's Spirit is saying to you? Are you noticing the way the Spirit is guiding you and providing you with wisdom? Or are you looking "out there somewhere"?

Here's the truth, friend. We make things much harder than they have to be. We believe that all will be well if we could just be better, or if we could do more for God, or pray more. We continue to berate ourselves and beat ourselves up over what we're not doing rather than focusing on the only things that really matter.

But the truth is that all God asks is that we believe in Him, love Him, and obey Him. That's it.

Believe in Him.

Love Him.

Obey Him.

Do those three things, and you will be set apart.

When belief, love, and obedience form the foundation of your relationship with God, you'll be more inclined to hear the Holy Spirit's gentle whispers, and you'll no longer live as the world does.

> Sometimes we expect an earthquake, and we miss his whisper. We expect a divine smack in the head, so we're oblivious to the divinity in the touch of our child's hand in ours as we cross the street.
>
> Our perception, or misperception, of God can distort his voice. If you want to hear God's whisper, begin by paying attention to who He really is and who you see yourself to be in relationship to Him.[11]

Our task as women going forward is to continually learn about who God is and to understand ourselves in relation to Him. Every experience we have, every challenge we overcome, and every bout of confusion we muddle through teaches us more about His character—and shapes ours in relation to Him.

Above all, hold onto this truth: Life is a journey designed to teach us about our Creator and to help us grow closer to Him. As you grow closer to Him, your walk becomes steadier, your confidence greater, and your gratitude deeper. Your walk with Him will become bold and joyful—an eagerly anticipated adventure between God and you, His precious child.

Know that He loves you and that He is enough to see you through. God has always been changing the world, one woman at a time.

Live the
DREAM

God is enough in every season and circumstance.

JOURNAL
PROMPTS

- What does the phrase "God is enough" mean to you?
- If you're more focused on living your dream than you are on God, how can you rearrange your priorities so that you're focusing on knowing God first?
- How does the idea of simplifying life to believing in God, loving Him, and obeying Him affect you?
- Are you ready to step out and journey forth as an extraordinary woman?

Conclusion

Extraordinary women come in all shapes and sizes. They come from varying backgrounds and experiences. But they all have one thing in common. They are allowing God to use who they are and where they are to make a difference for His kingdom.

When we close an Extraordinary Women conference, I love to share one of my favorite passages of the Bible. It is my prayer for you and over you. It's Jude 24-25 (NKJV): "Now to Him who is able to keep you from stumbling, and to present you faultless before the presence of His glory with exceeding joy, to God our Savior, who alone is wise, be glory and majesty, dominion and power, both now and forever. Amen."

May God go before you and fill your heart with Him. As you do all that you have to do each day, remember He is the wind beneath your wings. You are beautiful in His eyes.

So step out and journey forth. You're an extraordinary woman, and God is waiting to use you in ways you can't even begin to dream of!

Your girlfriend in Christ,
Julie

Notes

Chapter 1—Secrets to Living God's Dream for Your Life

1. Rick Warren, *The Purpose-Drive Life* (Grand Rapids: Zondervan, 2002), 243-244.

Chapter 2—Secrets to Knowing God Really Loves You

1. John and Stasi Eldredge, *Captivating* (Nashville: Thomas Nelson, 2005), 126.

2. Tim Clinton, *Turn Your Life Around* (New York: Faith Words, 2006), 139.

3. Miriam Dickinson, et al., "Health-Related Quality of Life and Symptom Profiles of Female Survivors of Sexual Abuse," *Archives of Family Medicine*, Jan-Feb 1999, p. 35. Available online at archfami.ama-assn.org/cgi/content/abstract/8/1/35. Lori Heise et al., "Ending Violence Against Women," *Population Reports*, Series L, No. 11. Johns Hopkins University School of Public Health, Population Information Program, December 1999. Available online at www.infoforhealth.org/pr/111/111creds.shtml#top.

4. Ernest Becker, *The Denial of Death* (New York: Free Press, 1973).

5. Sandra Guy, "Shopaholics, Take Heed," retrieved from hartfordadvocate.com/gbase/News/content?oid=oid:136964 on December 15, 2005.

6. Dallas Willard, *The Spirit of Disciplines* (San Francisco: Harper and Row, 1988), viii.

7. Joyce Meyer, *A Confident Woman* (New York: Warner Faith, 2006), 39-40.

8. "The Religious and Other Beliefs of Americans," HarrisInteractive. Available online at www.harrisinteractive.com/harris_poll/index.asp?PID=618.

9. Diane Langberg, "On Being Female," audio CD, Extraordinary Women Association, 2005.

Chapter 3—Secrets to Meaningful Relationships

1. Shankar Vedantam, "Social isolation growing in U.S., study says," *The Washington Post*, June 23, 2006, A03.

2. "Facts and Figures about our TV Habit," Center for Screen-Time Awareness. Available online at www.tvturnoff.org/images/facts&figs/factsheets/FactsFigs.pdf.

3. "Nearly Half of Our Lives Spent with TV, Radio, Internet, Newspapers," *United States Census Bureau News*, December 15, 2006. Available online at www.census.gov/Press-Release/www/releases/archives/miscellaneous/007871.html.

4. "The changing organization of work and the safety and health of working people," Centers for Disease Control and Prevention and National Institute for

Occupational Safety and Health, May 9, 2002. Available online at www.cdc.gov/niosh/pdfs/02-116.pdf.

5. "Finding Time," Yankelovich Monitor 2006/2007. Available online at www.yankelovich.com/time06/splash/time_splash.html.

6. Richard Swenson, *The Overload Syndrome* (Colorado Springs: NavPress, 1998), 125.

7. Everett Worthington, *Five Steps to Forgiveness* (New York: Crown Publishing, 2001), 18.

8. Ibid., 39.

9. Susan Cheever, "Heroes and Icons: Bill Wilson," *The Time 100,* June 14, 1999. Available online at www.time.com/time/time100/heroes/profile/wilson01.html.

10. "An Overview of Abortion in the United States," Guttmacher Institute. Available online at www.guttmacher.org/media/presskits/2005/06/28/abortionoverview.html.

11. Rachel K. Jones et al., "Repeat Abortion in the United States," Guttmacher Institute. Available online at www.guttmacher.org/pubs/2006/11/21/or29.pdf.

Chapter 4—Secrets to Handling Testosterone

1. Karen Scott Collins et al., "Health Concerns Across a Woman's Lifespan," The Commonwealth Fund, May 1999. Available online at www.cmwf.org/publications/publications_show.htm?doc_id=221554.

2. Bill and Pam Farrel, *Men Are Like Waffles, Women Are Like Spaghetti* (Eugene, Oregon: Harvest House Publishers, 2001), 11, 13.

3. Willard F. Harley, *His Needs, Her Needs* (Grand Rapids: Revell, 2001), 7.

4. Shaunti Feldhahn, personal e-mail, February 15, 2007.

5. Shaunti Feldhahn; *For Women Only* (Sisters, Oregon: Multnomah Publishers, 2004), 91-92.

6. Kevin Leman, *Sheet Music* (Wheaton, Illinois: Tyndale House Publishers, Inc., 2003), 46-53.

7. Gary and Barbara Rosberg, *The Five Sex Needs of Men and Women* (Carol Stream, Illinois: Tyndale House Publishers, Inc., 2006), 39.

8. Cited in Howard and Jeanne Hendricks, *Husbands and Wives* (Colorado Springs: Victor Books, 1988), 249.

Chapter 5—Secrets to Mastering Your Emotions

1. Lawrence J. Peter.

2. Michelle McKinney Hammond, personal e-mail, February 21, 2007.

3. "The Top Ten Fears That Keep People from Getting What They Want in Life." Available online at www.bgsu.edu/organizations/asc/Fears.pdf.

4. "Top Ten Phobias List." Available online at www.phobia-fear-release.com/top-ten-phobias.html.

5. List provided courtesy of Dr. Joseph Eby, pastor, Chatham Presbyterian Church, Chatham, Illinois.

6. "Let's Talk Facts About Depression," American Psychiatric Association. Available online at www.healthyminds.org/multimedia/depression.pdf.

7. From Paul Taylor, "Are there biblical examples of depression and how to deal with it?" Eden Communications. Available online at: www.christiananswers.net/q-eden/depression-bible.html.

8. "My journey into the valley of panic attacks, anxiety and depression." Available online at www.outreachofhope.org/index.cfm/PageID/362.

9. *The American Heritage Dictionary of the English Language, Fourth Edition.* Houghton Mifflin Company, 2004.

10. Henry Blackaby, *Reflections on the Seven Realities of Experiencing God* (Nashville: Broadman & Holman, 2001), as quoted in Henry Blackaby, "Watch God Work!" *Today's Christian Woman,* March/April 2002, 34.

Chapter 6—Secrets to Handling Imbalance

1. Joanna Weaver, *Having a Mary Heart in a Martha World* (Colorado Springs: WaterBrook Press, 2002), 102.

2. Cited in *Motherhood One Day at a Time* (Bloomington, Illinois: Hearts at Home, 2006), January 7.

3. Weaver, *Having a Mary Heart in a Martha World,* 9.

4. Stephen Covey, *The Seven Habits of Highly Effective People* (New York: Simon & Schuster, 1989), 241.

5. Don Piper and Cecil Murphey, *90 Minutes in Heaven* (Grand Rapids: Revell, 2004), 25-26.

6. "Stress in the Workplace," The American Institute of Stress. Available online at www.stress.org/Stress_in_the_workplace.htm.

7. Cited in John Schwartz, "Always on the job, employees pay with health," *New York Times,* September 5, 2004.

8. John Schwartz, "Sick of work," *The New York Times,* September 5, 2004.

9. Porter Anderson, "Study: U.S. employees put in most hours," CNN.com, August 31, 2001. Available online at archives.cnn.com/2001/CAREER/trends/08/30/ilo.study.

Chapter 7—Secrets to Getting Through Tough Times

1. A.W. Tozer, *Gems from Tozer* (Camp Hill, Pennsylvania: Christian Publications, 1979), 85.

2. Henri Nouwen, *Turn My Mourning into Dancing* (Nashville: Word Publishing, 2002), 10.

3. Ibid.

4. Lois Evans, "A Message of Hope," DVD, Extraordinary Women Association, 2006.

5. Carol Kent, personal communication, February 16, 2007.

6. Keri Wyatt Kent, personal communication.

7. Nouwen, *Turn My Mourning into Dancing*, 60.

8. Joni Eareckson Tada, personal communication, January 18, 2007.

9. Nouwen, *Turn My Mourning into Dancing*, 36.

10. J.I. Packer, *Knowing God* (Downers Grove, Illinois: InterVarsity Press, 1993), 227.

Chapter 8—Secrets to Finding Freedom

1. Bill and Kathy Peel, *Discover Your Destiny* (Colorado Springs: NavPress, 1997), 202.

2. Liz Curtis Higgs, *Mad Mary* (Colorado Springs: WaterBrook Press, 2001), 235-236.

3. Richard Swenson, *Margin* (Colorado Springs: NavPress, 2004), 116-117.

4. Karon Phillips Goodman, *You're Late Again, Lord* (Uhrichsville, Ohio: Barbour Publishing, 2002), 90.

5. Tim Clinton, *Turn Your Life Around* (Nashville: Faith Words, 2006), 168.

6. Goodman, *You're Late Again, Lord*, 79.

7. Cindy Crosby, "The Edge of Expectation," *Today's Christian Woman*, January/February 2004, 40-42.

8. Julie Barnhill, *Radical Forgiveness* (Wheaton, Illinois: Tyndale House Publishers, Inc., 2004), 37.

9. Liberty Savard, *Shattering Your Strongholds* (Orlando: Bridge-Logos Publishers, 1992), 35.

10. Clinton, *Turn Your Life Around*, 164.

11. Angela Thomas Guffey, *Tender Mercy for a Mother's Soul* (Wheaton, Illinois: Tyndale House Publishers, 2001), 35.

12. Doris R. Leckey, *7 Essentials for the Spiritual Journey* (New York: The Crossroad Publishing Company, 1999), 115.

13. Ibid., 111.

14. Liz Curtis Higgs, *Really Bad Girls of the Bible* (Colorado Springs: WaterBrook, 2000), 243.

Chapter 9—Secrets to Creating an Intimate Relationship with God

1. Donald Miller, *Blue Like Jazz* (Nashville: Thomas Nelson, 2003), 237.

2. Keri Wyatt Kent, *Oxygen* (Grand Rapids: Revell, 2007), 20-21.

3.   Walter Wangerin, *Whole Prayer* (Grand Rapids: Zondervan, 1998), 29.

4.   Tim Clinton and Gary Sibcy, *Why You Do the Things You Do* (Nashville: Integrity Publishers, 2006), 129.

5.   Erwin McManus, *Uprising* (Nashville: Thomas Nelson, 2003), 32.

6.   Oswald Chambers, *My Utmost for His Highest* (Uhrichsville, Ohio: Barbour Publishing, 2006), January 11.

7.   Aimee Lee Ball, "The Hallelujah Chorus," *Oprah,* December 2006, 310-312, 353-354.

8.   Ibid., 354.

9.   McManus, *Uprising,* 34.

Chapter 10—Secrets to Making Every Day Count

1.   A.W. Tozer, *Gems from Tozer* (Camp Hill, Pennsylvania: Christian Publications, 1969), 43-44.

2.   Tim Clinton and Gary Sibcy, *Why You Do the Things You Do* (Nashville: Integrity Publishers, 2006), 23.

3.   Tim Clinton, *Turn Your Life Around* (New York: Faith Words, 2006), 103.

4.   Ibid., 176.

5.   Tim Clinton, *National Liberty Journal,* May 1977, vol. 26, no. 5.

6.   Phil Vischer, *Me, Myself, and Bob* (Nashville: Nelson Books, 2006), 243-244.

7.   Tim Clinton and Gary Sibcy, *Loving Your Child Too Much* (Nashville: Integrity Publishers, 2006), 239.

8.   George Barna, *The Second Coming of the Church* (Nashville: Word Publishing, 1998), 7.

9.   J.I. Packer, *Knowing God* (Downers Grove, Illinois: InterVarsity Press, 1973), 209.

10.   Brent Curtis and John Eldredge, *The Sacred Romance* (Nashville: Thomas Nelson Publishers, 1997), 162.

11.   Keri Wyatt Kent, *God's Whisper in a Mother's Chaos* (Downers Grove, Illinois: InterVarsity Press, 2000), 25.

Other Great Harvest House Reading for Women

HOW TO SAY NO...AND LIVE TO TELL ABOUT IT
Mary Byers

Do you feel pressured to say yes to activities regardless of available time and resources? Mary offers strategies for quickly evaluating commitments, priorities, and energy levels so you can realistically decide what to do.

BECOMING A WOMAN WHO LISTENS TO GOD
Sharon Jaynes

Sharon Jaynes warmly invites readers to believe that they can hear God right in the middle of their busy lives as they engage in listening to the One who loves to talk to them.

THE POWER OF A PRAYING® WOMAN
Stormie Omartian

Bestselling author Stormie Omartian's deep knowledge of Scripture and examples from her own life provide guidance as you seek to trust God, maintain a right heart, and give your life over to God's purpose.

THE DIVA PRINCIPLE®
Michelle McKinney Hammond

Divine **I**nspiration for a **V**ictorious **A**ttitude...Michelle McKinney Hammond serves up the 4-1-1 on how to get and keep a victorious attitude—one entrenched in divine wisdom. She shows you how to excel in every area of life by mastering the art of diva-tude!

A WOMAN'S SECRET TO A BALANCED LIFE
Lysa Terkeurst and Sharon Jaynes

From the leadership of Proverbs 31 Ministries comes this essential book, offering seven vital ways you can prioritize your life more effectively.

HARVEST HOUSE
PUBLISHERS